Betty Crocker's
Casserole Cookbook

Director of Photography: Remo Cosentino
Illustrator: Tom Catania

Golden Press • New York
Western Publishing Company, Inc.
Racine, Wisconsin

REVISED EDITION
Second Printing This Edition, 1985
Copyright © 1984, 1981 by General Mills, Inc., Minneapolis, Minn.
All rights reserved. Produced in the U.S.A.
Library of Congress Catalog Card Number: 83-82256
Golden® and Golden Press® are trademarks of Western Publishing Company, Inc.
ISBN 0-307-09946-6

Casseroles are favorite fare—for family, for company, for streamlined menu-planning, for easy preparation, for quick cleanup. There's little or no watching involved, so you're free to do anything else that needs doing.

Whatever your taste preferences, whatever the occasion, you're sure to find the just-right recipe in this collection. We've included tried-and-true favorites like Beef Burgundy and Lasagne. And new flavor medleys like Hawaiian Halibut, Cheesy Eggs and Mushrooms and Taco Casserole. There are simple put-togethers like Baked Beans with Frankfurters and elegant combinations like Chicken with Phyllo.

But here's the special Betty Crocker "touch": All of these recipes were specifically developed to fit the needs of—and demands on—today's busy cooks. We know there are days when you simply don't want to heat up the kitchen, so many of the recipes feature top-of-the-range alternatives. We know that some days you need to speed up the cooking time, so we've included microwave directions wherever feasible. We know, too, that many of you like to cook in advance to cut down on preparation time, and so you'll find do-ahead notes to guide you. And be sure to familiarize yourself with the introductory pages for information about casserole dishes and using your microwave.

An important word about "servings": We're very much aware of the fact that protein is important for body-building and repair, but we're equally aware of the fact that the protein intake of most Americans is much greater than what is required. As a result, too many of us may be skimping on other foods (vegetables, fruits, breads, cereals, dairy products) that are just as necessary for a balanced diet. For this reason, we have planned our servings to provide about one-fourth of the day's protein requirement for an adult. (Remember, other foods usually eaten at mealtime also provide protein.) Therefore, even though the "servings" for some recipes may seem small to you, we assure you they are nutritionally adequate for protein. If you or members of your family have heartier appetites, figure on fewer servings per recipe.

Betty Crocker

Contents

4 About Casseroles

7 Meat Casseroles

41 Poultry Casseroles

59 Fish & Seafood Casseroles

75 Egg, Cheese & Bean Casseroles

93 Index

About Casseroles

A casserole is a casserole is a casserole. Or is it? To the French, the term "casserole" means the cooking container *and* what's cooked in it. For Americans, "casserole" has taken on the added meaning of a one-dish meal.

What goes in this one dish can range from simple threesomes all the way to myriad mixtures. But for a casserole to qualify as a true main dish it must combine protein (meat, poultry, seafood, eggs, dried beans or cheese) with a starchy ingredient (rice, pasta, vegetable or bread); a sauce or gravy often provides the meld. To add color, texture or flavor, you can top the whole affair, as appropriate, with cheese, bread crumbs, croutons, chopped nuts or crushed cereals or crackers. Or you can take a sturdier route with toppers of biscuits, corn bread or dumplings.

TAKE YOUR PICK

With so many sizes, shapes and kinds of casserole dishes for sale, profusion can lead to confusion. Look for sizes that "fit" most recipes. Then check out features like storability, easy-care finishes, oven-to-table use and overall attractiveness. But don't blow the budget for beauty. You can camouflage even the most mundane container with a good-looking basket or metal casserole holder. To help you decide which type of casserole is best for you, check the chart below.

Type of Ovenware	Advantages	What to Look For
Oven-to-table baking dishes (ovenproof glass, enameled metal, stoneware, etc.).	Versatile. Cuts down on dishwashing. Wide choice of styles.	Covered dishes are most useful. Should withstand broiler heat for top browning.
Ovenproof skillets and Dutch ovens.	Multipurpose; for range-top and oven.	Tight-fitting lids, ovenproof knobs and handles.
Refrigerator/freezer-to-range-to-table pieces.	Tops for versatility. Almost indestructible.	Tight-fitting lids (or you can use aluminum foil).

P.S.   Always follow any special instructions from the manufacturer.

FOR BEST RESULTS

Try, as best you can, to match the size and shape casserole that's called for in the recipe. Too large a dish allows too much moisture to evaporate, leaving the food dry; too small a dish tempts the food to bubble over. Go too deep and the food might be undercooked and, just the reverse, go too shallow and you'll have overcooked and/or burned food.

To avoid these pitfalls, know how much your casserole can hold. A casserole is measured in volume: 1 quart, 2 quarts and so on. If you don't know and it's not marked, determine the volume by filling the dish to the brim with measured amounts of water. The size of a baking dish or pan is indicated by dimensions, such as 13x9x2 inches. To check the size, measure across the top from the *inside* edges— first the length and width, then the inside bottom to top for depth.

Most of the recipes in this book give both the recommended casserole and baking dish sizes, so you would know, for example, that the capacity of a 13x9x2-inch baking dish equals that of a 3-quart casserole. For other recipes, here's a helpful conversion table:

Baking Dish and Pan Sizes

Dimensions	Volume
9x9x2 inches	2½ quarts
8x8x2 inches	2 quarts
13x9x2 inches	3 quarts
12x7½x2 inches	2 quarts
10x6x1½ inches	1½ quarts

OVEN OR TOP OF THE RANGE?

Although all of the recipes in this book have been developed and tested for the oven, whenever feasible, range-top, microwave and do-ahead instructions have been included to add versatility. Even though oven dishes need little if any "looking after," there are times when microwave or top-of-the-range preparation might be more convenient—not to mention those occasions when there is no time for preparation and the do-ahead directions become a necessity.

Cooking Tips and Energy Savers

Oven:
■ When using one oven rack, try to position it so the oven space above and below the casserole is the same.

■ When using two oven racks, try to divide the oven space into thirds. When there's more than one pan, for good heat circulation, stagger pans so that one is not directly over another.

■ A casserole should never touch the side of the oven or the side of another pan. A clearance of 1½ to 2 inches all around will let air circulate properly for even cooking.

■ Oven temperatures can vary a bit, so check for doneness when the minimum time has elapsed—especially the first time you try a recipe.

■ Preheat the oven only when specified. Most casseroles can start in a cold oven.

Range:
■ Use flat-bottomed pans of medium weight for even, quick heat conduction.

■ With gas, adjust the flame to the pan size; with electric, fit the heating unit to the size of the pan.

■ Use the lowest setting possible to achieve the desired cooking method. Turning the heat up and down can create hot spots and cause sticking.

TEMPERAMENTAL THERMOSTATS

Even thermostats can get cranky; so it's a good idea to check out oven temperatures every so often. Place an oven thermometer on a centered rack, then wait 10 to 15 minutes and compare the actual oven temperature to the setting on the oven control. Try another temperature and make the same comparison. If the thermostat is off, adjust the setting accordingly until the necessary repair can be made.

OVEN CLEANING TIPS

■ Sprinkle salt on any spill-overs as soon as you can. Chances are you'll be able to lift or brush them out easily when the oven cools.

■ Keep your oven clean by wiping the still-warm walls with a cloth wrung out in a mild solution of water and vinegar or baking soda. If you can't or don't get to it, eventually you'll have to use a commercial oven cleaner. They do the job but they are strong, so follow the directions to the letter.

ON ANOTHER WAVELENGTH—MICROWAVE

Let's face it, there's nothing faddy or futuristic about microwaves anymore. There's no attempt here to provide a mini-course on micro-waving; rather the intent is simply to give you a good frame of reference for the microwave directions included in this book.

■ All the microwave directions were tested in counter-top microwaves with outputs of 600 to 700 watts. A variety of brands and models was used. Although they had different features and power levels, to minimize these differences all recipes specify a percentage setting such as 100% or 50% power. Of course, for best results use the power setting specified in the recipe.

■ If your microwave has an output of less than 600 watts, some increase in the suggested cooking times may be necessary.

■ Although there are many specially developed "microwave-suitable" products on the market, chances are you have plenty of usable utensils on hand. Oven-tempered glassware leads the list along with ceramic casseroles, providing they contain no metal. (Metal, as you know, is a problem for microwaves.) If you have any doubt about any of your containers, test them. To test any dish, place 1 cup water in a glass measure and set it in or beside the container. If the container becomes warm after 1 minute at 100%, don't use it in your microwave.

■ Microwave timings are trickier than you might expect. The cooking times specified are as accurate *an average* as possible since you are cooking at a much faster pace. Cook to the minimum time the first time round—you can always add another minute or so.

■ Coverings are often used to keep moisture in and to prevent liquid foods from spattering. In the following microwave recipes "cover tightly" means that no steam or moisture should escape. Use a snug-fitting casserole lid or rest a plate on top. If using a baking dish, cover with plastic wrap, turning back one edge to vent. "Cover loosely" means that a certain amount of moisture and steam should be permitted to escape. Use waxed paper or a paper towel as the covering. "Uncovered" means just that—foods that have dry surfaces, need frequent attention or benefit from evaporation should not be covered.

■ Because the microwaves bounce around the cavity in random patterns, foods often cook faster in one area than in another. Therefore, it is sometimes necessary to rotate the dish, to stir the food or even to let it stand for awhile in order to even out the cooking. When directed, turn dishes a quarter-turn midway through the cooking period. When stirring, stir from the outside edges (where the food is hotter) toward the center. A "standing time" after microwaving helps equalize the heat and blend the flavors.

SERVING TIME!

All the good things like eggs, milk, seafood, meat and poultry that go into casseroles also tend to make them more perishable than some other foods. Once your casserole is cooked, serve it right away or keep it hot until ready. If you're cooking ahead, refrigerate the dish as soon as possible. Standing at room temperature for more than 2 hours can encourage the growth of harmful bacteria. These microorganisms can spoil food without a change of taste, odor or appearance. Be smart and follow United States Department of Agriculture advice that hot foods should be kept hot (above 140°F.) and cold foods should be kept cold (below 40°F.).

Meat Casseroles

CHOP SUEY CASSEROLE

 1 pound ground beef
 ¾ cup chopped celery
 3 tablespoons instant minced
      onion
1¼ cups water
 ½ cup uncooked converted rice
 ½ teaspoon salt
 1 can (10½ ounces) condensed
      chicken with rice soup
 1 can (4 ounces) mushroom stems
      and pieces, drained
 1 tablespoon packed brown sugar
 2 tablespoons soy sauce
 1 teaspoon margarine or butter

Cook and stir ground beef, celery and onion in 10-inch skillet until beef is brown; drain. Stir in remaining ingredients.

OVEN METHOD: Pour into greased 2-quart casserole or 12x7½x2-inch baking dish. Cook uncovered in 350° oven 30 minutes; stir. Cook until rice is tender and liquid is absorbed, about 30 minutes longer.

RANGE-TOP METHOD: Heat to boiling; reduce heat. Cover and simmer, stirring occasionally, until rice is tender and liquid is absorbed, about 30 minutes.

4 or 5 servings.

CURRIED BEEF AND RICE

1½ pounds ground beef
 1 medium onion, sliced
 1 cup uncooked regular rice
2½ cups water
 2 teaspoons instant chicken
      bouillon
 1 teaspoon curry powder
 ½ teaspoon salt
 ¼ teaspoon ground ginger
 ¼ teaspoon ground cinnamon
 3 tablespoons peanut butter
 1 tablespoon honey
 ½ cup raisins

Cook and stir ground beef and onion in 10-inch skillet until beef is brown; drain. Stir in remaining ingredients.

OVEN METHOD: Pour into ungreased 2-quart casserole or 12x7½x2-inch baking dish. Cover and cook in 350° oven, stirring occasionally, until rice is tender and liquid is absorbed, 50 to 60 minutes. (Add small amount water if necessary.)

RANGE-TOP METHOD: Heat to boiling; reduce heat. Cover and simmer, stirring occasionally, until rice is tender and liquid is absorbed, about 35 minutes. (Add small amount water if necessary.)

8 servings.

TEXAS HASH

1 pound ground beef
3 large onions, sliced
1 large green pepper, chopped
    (about 1½ cups)
1 can (16 ounces) whole tomatoes
½ cup uncooked regular rice
2 teaspoons salt
1 to 2 teaspoons chili powder
⅛ teaspoon pepper

Cook and stir ground beef, onions and green pepper in 10-inch skillet until beef is brown; drain. Stir in tomatoes (with liquid) and the remaining ingredients.

OVEN METHOD: Pour into ungreased 2-quart casserole or 12x7½x2-inch baking dish. Cover and cook in 350° oven until rice is tender and liquid is absorbed, about 1 hour.

RANGE-TOP METHOD: Heat to boiling; reduce heat. Cover and simmer, stirring occasionally, until rice is tender and liquid is absorbed, about 30 minutes.

6 servings.

■ To Microwave: Crumble ground beef into 3-quart microwaveproof casserole; add onions and green pepper. Cover tightly and microwave on high (100%) 4 minutes; break up and stir. Cover and microwave until vegetables are tender, 4 to 6 minutes longer; drain. Stir in tomatoes (with liquid), ¾ cup uncooked instant rice, the salt, chili powder and pepper. Cover tightly and microwave 5 minutes; stir. Cover and microwave until rice is almost tender, 4 to 6 minutes longer. Let stand 5 minutes.

HEARTY BEEF CASSEROLE

1½ pounds ground beef
  1 large onion, chopped (about 1
    cup)
  2 medium tomatoes, chopped
    (about 2 cups)
  2 cups water
  1 cup uncooked bulgur wheat
  3 tablespoons snipped parsley
  2 teaspoons instant beef bouillon
1½ teaspoons salt
  ½ teaspoon dried oregano leaves
  ¼ teaspoon instant minced garlic
  ¼ teaspoon pepper
  ½ cup grated Parmesan cheese

Cook and stir ground beef and onion in 10-inch skillet until beef is brown; drain. Stir in remaining ingredients except cheese.

OVEN METHOD: Pour into ungreased 2-quart casserole or 12x7½x2-inch baking dish. Cover and cook in 350° oven until wheat is tender, about 45 minutes. Stir in cheese. Sprinkle with additional Parmesan cheese and snipped parsley if desired.

RANGE-TOP METHOD: Heat to boiling; reduce heat. Cover and simmer, stirring occasionally, until wheat is tender, about 30 minutes. (Add small amount water if necessary.) Stir in cheese. Sprinkle with additional Parmesan cheese and snipped parsley if desired.

7 servings.

■ To Microwave: Crumble ground beef into 3-quart microwaveproof casserole; add onion. Cover loosely and microwave on high (100%) 5 minutes; break up and stir. Cover and microwave until very little pink remains, 4 to 6 minutes longer; drain. Stir in remaining ingredients except cheese. Cover tightly and microwave 10 minutes; stir. Cover and microwave until wheat is tender, 10 to 14 minutes longer. Stir in cheese. Sprinkle with additional Parmesan cheese and snipped parsley if desired.

BEEF AND EGGPLANT CASSEROLE

1 pound ground beef
1 small eggplant (about 1 pound), cut into 1-inch pieces (about 5 cups)
1 cup uncooked elbow spaghetti (about 3 ounces)
½ cup water
1 clove garlic, finely chopped
1 tablespoon salt
1 teaspoon dried oregano leaves
¼ teaspoon pepper
4 medium tomatoes, each cut into fourths
2 medium onions, coarsely chopped (about 2 cups)
1 medium green pepper, cut into strips
¼ cup grated Parmesan cheese

Cook and stir ground beef in 4-quart Dutch oven until brown; drain. Stir in eggplant, spaghetti, water, garlic, salt, oregano and pepper.

OVEN METHOD: Pour into ungreased 3-quart casserole or 13x9x2-inch baking dish. Top with tomatoes, onions and green pepper. Cover and cook in 350° oven until eggplant is tender, 50 to 60 minutes. Stir; sprinkle with cheese. Serve with additional Parmesan cheese if desired.

RANGE-TOP METHOD: Heat to boiling, stirring constantly; reduce heat. Top with tomatoes, onions and green pepper. Cover and simmer, stirring occasionally, until spaghetti is tender and vegetables are crisp-tender, 20 to 25 minutes. Stir; sprinkle with cheese. Serve with additional Parmesan cheese if desired.

6 to 8 servings.

Beef and Eggplant Casserole showcases a hearty harvest of vegetables.

GREEN BEAN-MUSHROOM MEDLEY

1 pound ground beef
1 medium onion, chopped (about ½ cup)
1 can (16 ounces) green beans
1 can (10¾ ounces) condensed cream of mushroom soup
1 can (4 ounces) mushroom stems and pieces, drained
1 small green pepper, chopped (about ½ cup)
1 medium stalk celery, chopped (about ½ cup)
1 cup milk
1 tablespoon Worcestershire sauce
1 teaspoon salt
2 cups uncooked egg noodles

Cook and stir ground beef and onion in 12-inch skillet or 4-quart Dutch oven until beef is brown; drain. Stir in beans (with liquid) and the remaining ingredients.

OVEN METHOD: Pour into ungreased 2-quart casserole or 12x7½x2-inch baking dish. Cover and cook in 350° oven until noodles are tender, about 35 minutes.

RANGE-TOP METHOD: Heat to boiling; reduce heat. Cover and simmer, stirring occasionally, until noodles are tender, 25 to 30 minutes.

6 to 8 servings.

Green Bean-Tomato Medley: Omit mushrooms and milk. Stir in 1 can (28 ounces) whole tomatoes (with liquid) and ½ cup catsup with the remaining ingredients.

■ **To Microwave:** Crumble ground beef into 3-quart microwaveproof casserole; add onion. Cover loosely and microwave on high (100%) 3 minutes; break up and stir. Cover and microwave until very little pink remains, 2 to 3 minutes longer; drain. Stir in beans (with liquid) and the remaining ingredients. Cover tightly and microwave 8 minutes; stir. Cover and microwave until noodles are almost tender, 8 to 12 minutes longer; stir. Cover and let stand 5 minutes.

CRUNCHY BEEF-NOODLE CASSEROLE

1 pound ground beef
1 large onion, chopped (about ¾ cup)
1 can (10¾ ounces) condensed cream of chicken soup
1 can (4 ounces) mushroom stems and pieces
¾ cup milk
1 small green pepper, chopped
½ cup sliced pitted ripe olives
2 tablespoons soy sauce
2 teaspoons Worcestershire sauce
⅛ teaspoon pepper
5 ounces egg noodles, cooked and drained
1 cup shredded sharp Cheddar or process American cheese (about 4 ounces)
1 cup chow mein noodles
½ cup mixed salted nuts

Cook and stir ground beef and onion in 10-inch skillet until beef is brown; drain. Stir in soup, mushrooms (with liquid), milk, green pepper, olives, soy sauce, Worcestershire sauce, pepper and egg noodles. Pour into ungreased 2-quart casserole; sprinkle with cheese. Cover and cook in 350° oven 50 minutes. Top with chow mein noodles and nuts; cook uncovered 10 minutes.

6 to 8 servings.

Do-ahead Note: After sprinkling with cheese, cover and refrigerate no longer than 24 hours. To serve, cook covered in 350° oven 50 minutes. Top with chow mein noodles and nuts; cook uncovered 10 minutes.

BEEF AND MACARONI

      1 package (7 ounces) elbow
            macaroni
      1 pound ground beef
      1 medium onion, chopped (about
            ½ cup)
      1 can (8 ounces) tomato sauce
      ½ teaspoon dried oregano leaves
      ¼ teaspoon salt
      ¼ teaspoon ground cinnamon
      ⅛ teaspoon ground nutmeg
      1 large clove garlic, crushed
      2 tablespoons margarine or butter
      2 tablespoons all-purpose flour
      ¼ teaspoon salt
         Dash of ground nutmeg
   1 ½ cups milk
      ¼ cup grated Romano cheese

Cook macaroni as directed on package; drain. Cook and stir ground beef and onion in 10-inch skillet until beef is brown; drain. Stir in tomato sauce, oregano, ¼ teaspoon salt, the cinnamon, ⅛ teaspoon nutmeg and the garlic. Alternate layers of macaroni and beef mixture in ungreased 2-quart casserole.

Heat margarine in 1-quart saucepan over low heat until melted. Stir in flour, ¼ teaspoon salt and dash of nutmeg. Cook over low heat, stirring constantly, until smooth and bubbly; remove from heat. Stir in milk. Heat to boiling, stirring constantly. Boil and stir 1 minute. Spoon sauce over macaroni and beef mixture; sprinkle with cheese. Cook uncovered in 350° oven until bubbly and cheese is light brown, about 35 minutes.

6 servings.

CHILI WITH MACARONI

      1 pound ground beef
      2 medium onions, chopped (about
            1 cup)
      1 large green pepper, chopped
            (about 1 cup)
      1 can (28 ounces) whole tomatoes
      1 can (15½ ounces) kidney beans
      1 can (8 ounces) tomato sauce
      1 cup uncooked elbow macaroni
            (about 3 ounces)
      2 to 4 teaspoons chili powder
      1 teaspoon salt
      ⅛ teaspoon cayenne pepper
      ⅛ teaspoon paprika

Cook and stir ground beef, onions and green pepper in 10-inch skillet until beef is brown; drain. Stir in tomatoes (with liquid), beans (with liquid) and the remaining ingredients.

OVEN METHOD: Pour into ungreased 3-quart casserole or 13x9x2-inch baking dish. Cover and cook in 350° oven until macaroni is tender, about 45 minutes.

RANGE-TOP METHOD: Heat to boiling; reduce heat. Cover and simmer, stirring occasionally, until macaroni is tender, 20 to 30 minutes.

6 to 8 servings.

■ **To Microwave:** Crumble ground beef into 3-quart microwaveproof casserole; add onions and green pepper. Cover tightly and microwave on high (100%) 4 minutes; stir. Cover and microwave until very little pink remains, 3 to 4 minutes longer; drain. Stir in remaining ingredients. Cover tightly and microwave, stirring every 5 minutes, until macaroni is tender, 20 to 23 minutes.

EASY OVEN SPAGHETTI

1 pound ground beef
2 medium onions, chopped (about 1 cup)
1 can (28 ounces) whole tomatoes
¾ cup chopped green pepper
½ cup water
1 can (4 ounces) mushroom stems and pieces, drained
2 teaspoons salt
1 teaspoon sugar
1 teaspoon chili powder
1 package (7 ounces) thin spaghetti, broken into 2-inch pieces
1 cup shredded Cheddar or process American cheese (about 4 ounces)

Cook and stir ground beef and onions in 10-inch skillet or 4-quart Dutch oven until beef is brown; drain. Stir in tomatoes (with liquid) and the remaining ingredients except cheese; break up tomatoes with fork.

OVEN METHOD: Pour into ungreased 2- or 2½-quart casserole or 12x7½x2-inch baking dish. Cover and cook in 375° oven, stirring occasionally, until spaghetti is tender, about 45 minutes. Sprinkle with cheese. Cook uncovered until cheese is melted, about 5 minutes.

RANGE-TOP METHOD: Heat to boiling; reduce heat. Cover and simmer, stirring occasionally, until spaghetti is tender, about 30 minutes. (Add small amount water if necessary.) Sprinkle with cheese. Cover and heat until cheese is melted.

7 servings.

■ **To Microwave:** Crumble ground beef into 3-quart microwaveproof casserole; add onions. Cover tightly and microwave on high (100%) 3 minutes; stir. Cover and microwave until very little pink remains, 3 to 4 minutes longer; drain. Stir in tomatoes (with liquid) and the remaining ingredients except cheese; break up tomatoes with fork. Cover tightly and microwave, stirring every 5 minutes, until spaghetti is tender, 18 to 21 minutes. Sprinkle with cheese. Cover and let stand 5 minutes.

BEEF MANICOTTI

1 pound ground beef
1 small onion, chopped (about ¼ cup)
3 slices bread, torn into small pieces
1½ cups shredded mozzarella cheese (about 6 ounces)
1 egg
½ cup milk
1 tablespoon snipped parsley
1 teaspoon salt
¼ teaspoon pepper
1 package (8 ounces) manicotti shells
1 can (4 ounces) mushroom stems and pieces
1 can (15 ounces) tomato sauce
1 can (12 ounces) tomato paste
1 small onion, chopped (about ¼ cup)
1 clove garlic, finely chopped
4 cups water
1 tablespoon Italian seasoning
½ teaspoon sugar
½ teaspoon salt
⅛ teaspoon pepper
⅓ cup grated Parmesan cheese

Cook and stir ground beef and ¼ cup onion in a 10-inch skillet until beef is brown; drain. Stir in bread, mozzarella cheese, egg, milk, parsley, 1 teaspoon salt and ¼ teaspoon pepper. Fill uncooked manicotti shells, packing beef mixture into both ends. Place shells in ungreased 13x9x2-inch pan.

Heat mushrooms (with liquid) and the remaining ingredients except Parmesan cheese to boiling, stirring occasionally; reduce heat. Simmer uncovered 5 minutes. Pour sauce over shells. Cover and cook in 375° oven until shells are tender, 1½ to 1¾ hours. Sprinkle with cheese. Let stand 5 to 10 minutes before serving.

6 to 8 servings.

Do-ahead Note: After filling shells, wrap, label and freeze no longer than 2 months. To serve, unwrap frozen shells and place in ungreased 13x9x2-inch pan. Prepare tomato sauce; pour over shells. Cover and cook in 375° oven until shells are tender, 1¾ to 2 hours.

BEEF AND POTATO STRATA

2½ cups water
1 package (5.5 ounces) au gratin
   potato mix
2 pounds ground beef
1 medium onion, chopped (about
   ½ cup)
1 can (16 ounces) whole tomatoes
1 can (8 ounces) tomato sauce or
   pizza sauce
1 teaspoon salt
1 teaspoon dried oregano leaves
½ teaspoon dried basil leaves
⅛ teaspoon garlic powder
1 cup creamed cottage cheese
   (small curd)
2 cups shredded mozzarella cheese
   (about 8 ounces)
½ cup grated Parmesan cheese

Heat water to boiling; add potatoes. Cook until water is absorbed. Cook and stir ground beef and onion in 10-inch skillet until beef is brown; drain. Stir in Sauce Mix, tomatoes (with liquid), tomato sauce, salt, oregano, basil and garlic powder; break up tomatoes with fork. Simmer uncovered 20 minutes.

Reserve 1 cup beef mixture. Spread 1 cup of the remaining beef mixture in greased 13x9x2-inch baking dish. Top with half of the potatoes, half of the remaining beef mixture, ½ cup of the cottage cheese, 1 cup mozzarella cheese and ¼ cup of the Parmesan cheese. Repeat with remaining potatoes, beef mixture, cottage cheese and mozzarella cheese. Spread reserved beef mixture over top. Sprinkle with remaining Parmesan cheese. Cook uncovered in 350° oven 30 minutes. Let stand 10 minutes before cutting.

8 servings.

BROCCOLI-BEEF SQUARES

2 cups chopped fresh broccoli*
1 pound ground beef
1 can (4 ounces) mushroom stems
   and pieces, drained
2 cups shredded Cheddar cheese
   (about 8 ounces)
⅓ cup chopped onion
2 cups buttermilk baking mix
½ cup cold water
¼ cup grated Parmesan cheese
1 teaspoon salt
   Dash of pepper
½ cup milk
4 eggs

Heat 1 inch salted water (½ teaspoon salt to 1 cup water) to boiling. Add broccoli. Cover and heat to boiling. Cook until almost tender, about 5 minutes; drain thoroughly.

Cook and stir ground beef in 10-inch skillet until brown; drain. Stir in mushrooms, 1½ cups of the Cheddar cheese and the onion. Mix baking mix, water and the remaining Cheddar cheese until soft dough forms; beat vigorously 20 strokes. Pat dough in greased 13x9x2-inch baking dish with floured hands, pressing dough ½ inch up sides. Spread beef mixture over dough; sprinkle with broccoli. Mix remaining ingredients; pour over broccoli. Cook uncovered in 400° oven until golden brown and knife inserted near center comes out clean, 25 to 30 minutes.

6 to 8 servings.

*1 package (10 ounces) frozen chopped broccoli, thawed and drained, can be substituted for the fresh broccoli. Do not cook.

TACO CASSEROLE

1 pound ground beef
1 can (15 ounces) chili beans
1 can (8 ounces) tomato sauce
2 tablespoons taco sauce
2 to 4 teaspoons chili powder
1 teaspoon garlic salt
2 cups coarsely broken tortilla chips
1 cup dairy sour cream
½ cup sliced green onions (with
    tops)
1 tomato, chopped
1 cup shredded Cheddar or Monterey
    Jack cheese (about 4 ounces)

Cook and stir ground beef in 10-inch skillet until brown; drain. Stir in beans, tomato sauce, taco sauce, chili powder and garlic salt. Heat to boiling.

Place chips in ungreased 2-quart casserole or 12x7½x2-inch baking dish. Top with beef mixture. Spread with sour cream. Sprinkle with onions, tomato and cheese. Cook uncovered in 350° oven until hot and bubbly, 20 to 30 minutes. Arrange additional tortilla chips around edge of casserole. Serve with shredded lettuce, chili peppers and taco sauce if desired.

6 servings.

NO-NOODLE LASAGNE

1 pound ground beef
1 can (15 ounces) tomato sauce
1½ teaspoons garlic salt
1 teaspoon dried basil leaves
1 teaspoon dried oregano leaves
1½ cups dry cottage cheese (about
    12 ounces)
¼ cup grated Romano cheese
1 egg
1½ pounds zucchini, cut lengthwise
    into ¼-inch slices
2 tablespoons all-purpose flour
1 cup shredded mozzarella cheese
    (about 4 ounces)
¼ cup grated Romano cheese

Cook and stir ground beef in 10-inch skillet until brown; drain. Stir in tomato sauce, garlic salt, basil and oregano. Heat to boiling,

stirring occasionally; reduce heat. Simmer uncovered until consistency of spaghetti sauce, about 10 minutes.

Mix cottage cheese, ¼ cup Romano cheese and the egg. Layer half each of the zucchini, flour, cottage cheese mixture, sauce mixture and mozzarella cheese in ungreased 9x9x2-inch pan; repeat. Sprinkle ¼ cup Romano cheese on top. Cook uncovered in 350° oven until golden brown, about 45 minutes. Let stand 20 minutes before cutting.

9 servings.

IMPOSSIBLE CHEESEBURGER PIE

1 pound ground beef
1½ cups chopped onion
1½ cups milk
¾ cup buttermilk baking mix
3 eggs
½ teaspoon salt
¼ teaspoon pepper
2 tomatoes, sliced
1 cup shredded Cheddar or
    process American cheese
    (about 4 ounces)

Heat oven to 400°. Grease 10x1½-inch pie plate. Cook and stir ground beef and onion in 10-inch skillet until beef is brown; drain. Spread in pie plate. Beat milk, baking mix, eggs, salt and pepper until smooth, 15 seconds in blender on high speed or 1 minute with hand beater. Pour into pie plate. Bake 25 minutes. Top with tomatoes; sprinkle with cheese. Bake until knife inserted in center comes out clean, 5 to 8 minutes longer. Let stand 5 minutes before cutting. Refrigerate any remaining pie.

6 to 8 servings.

Pictured at right: A ring of tortilla chips echoes the bottom layer of Taco Casserole (this page), a zesty ground beef medley featuring south-of-the-border flavors.

CHEESE-TOPPED BEEF PIE

1 pound ground beef
1 small green pepper, chopped
(about ½ cup)
1 small onion, chopped (about
¼ cup)
1 jar (2 ounces) diced pimiento,
drained
½ cup all-purpose flour
½ cup milk
2 eggs, separated
1 egg
1 teaspoon salt
⅛ teaspoon pepper
1 tablespoon margarine or butter
1 tablespoon all-purpose flour
½ teaspoon dry mustard
¼ teaspoon salt
Dash of cayenne pepper
½ cup milk
1 cup shredded Cheddar cheese
(about 4 ounces)

Cook and stir ground beef, green pepper and onion in 10-inch skillet until beef is brown; drain. Stir in pimiento. Spread beef mixture in ungreased 9x1¼-inch pie plate. Beat ½ cup flour, ½ cup milk, the egg yolks, egg, 1 teaspoon salt and the pepper with hand beater until smooth. Pour over beef mixture in pie plate.

Heat oven to 375°. Heat margarine in 1-quart saucepan until melted. Stir in 1 tablespoon flour, the mustard, ¼ teaspoon salt and the cayenne pepper. Cook over low heat, stirring constantly, until smooth and bubbly; remove from heat. Stir in ½ cup milk. Heat to boiling, stirring constantly. Boil and stir 1 minute. Add cheese; cook and stir over low heat just until cheese is melted. Beat egg whites until stiff but not dry; fold in cheese mixture. Spread over beef mixture. Cook uncovered until golden brown and knife inserted halfway between center and edge comes out clean, 20 to 25 minutes. Serve immediately.

8 servings.

MEXICALI SPOON BREAD CASSEROLE

1½ pounds ground beef
1 large onion, chopped (about 1 cup)
½ small green pepper, chopped
1 clove garlic, finely chopped
1 can (15 ounces) tomato sauce
1 can (12 ounces) vacuum-pack
whole kernel corn
2 to 3 teaspoons chili powder
1½ teaspoons salt
⅛ teaspoon pepper
½ cup sliced ripe olives
1½ cups milk
½ cup yellow cornmeal
½ teaspoon salt
¾ cup shredded Cheddar cheese
2 eggs, beaten

Cook and stir ground beef, onion, green pepper and garlic in 10-inch skillet until beef is brown; drain. Stir in tomato sauce, corn (with liquid), chili powder, 1½ teaspoons salt, the pepper and olives. Heat to boiling; reduce heat.

Mix milk, cornmeal and ½ teaspoon salt in saucepan. Heat just to boiling over medium heat, stirring constantly; remove from heat. Stir in cheese and eggs. Pour hot beef mixture into ungreased 3-quart casserole or 13x9x2-inch baking dish. Immediately pour cornmeal mixture over top. Cook uncovered in 375° oven until knife inserted in topping comes out clean, about 40 minutes.

6 to 8 servings.

LAYERED TOSTADA BAKE

1 pound ground beef
1 medium onion, chopped (about
    ½ cup)
1 envelope (1¼ ounces) taco
    seasoning mix
1 can (8 ounces) tomato sauce
1 can (16 ounces) refried beans
1 can (4 ounces) whole green chilies,
    drained, seeded and chopped
½ cup sliced pitted ripe olives
1 cup buttermilk baking mix
½ cup cornmeal
¼ cup milk
1 egg, beaten
2 tablespoons vegetable oil
1 cup dairy sour cream
1 egg
2 cups shredded Cheddar cheese
    (about 8 ounces)

Heat oven to 375°. Grease 12x7½x2-inch baking dish. Cook and stir ground beef and onion in 10-inch skillet until beef is brown; drain. Stir in seasoning mix, tomato sauce, beans, chilies and olives. Mix baking mix, cornmeal, milk, beaten egg and oil until moistened; beat vigorously 30 seconds. Spread in dish. Spoon beef mixture over dough. Mix remaining ingredients; spoon over beef mixture. Cook uncovered 30 minutes. Let stand 10 minutes before cutting.

6 to 8 servings.

STROGANOFF DEEP DISH PIE

1 pound ground beef
1 medium onion, chopped (about
    ½ cup)
½ cup dairy sour cream
¼ cup catsup
2 eggs
1 can (10¾ ounces) condensed
    cream of mushroom soup
1 can (4 ounces) mushroom stems
    and pieces, drained
2 cups buttermilk baking mix
½ cup cold water

Heat oven to 375°. Cook and stir ground beef and onion in 10-inch skillet until beef is brown;

drain. Mix sour cream, catsup, eggs and soup with fork until well blended. Stir in beef mixture and mushrooms.

Mix baking mix and water until soft dough forms; beat vigorously 20 strokes. Pat dough in greased 13x9x2-inch pan with floured hands, pressing dough 1 inch up sides. Spread beef mixture over dough. Bake uncovered until crust is light brown and beef mixture is set, 25 to 30 minutes. Garnish with parsley if desired.

6 servings.

POPOVER-TOPPED BEEF

1 pound ground beef
1 can (15 ounces) tomato sauce
¼ cup chopped green pepper
2 tablespoons all-purpose flour
1 teaspoon parsley flakes
½ teaspoon salt
¼ teaspoon pepper
1 cup shredded Cheddar cheese
    (about 4 ounces)
2 eggs
1 cup milk
1 tablespoon vegetable oil
1 cup all-purpose flour
½ teaspoon salt
2 tablespoons chopped green onions

Cook and stir ground beef in 10-inch skillet until brown; drain. Stir in tomato sauce, green pepper, 2 tablespoons flour, the parsley, ½ teaspoon salt and the pepper. Heat to boiling, stirring constantly. Boil and stir 1 minute. Pour into ungreased 13x9x2-inch pan. Sprinkle cheese on top. Beat eggs, milk, oil, 1 cup flour and ½ teaspoon salt with hand beater until smooth; pour over cheese. Sprinkle with onions. Cook uncovered in 425° oven until golden brown, 25 to 30 minutes. Serve immediately.

6 servings.

MEATBALLS WITH MIXED VEGETABLES

1 package (10 ounces) frozen mixed
   vegetables*
1 egg
¼ cup milk
1 cup soft bread crumbs
1 teaspoon salt
½ teaspoon dry mustard
½ teaspoon celery salt
¼ teaspoon ground nutmeg
¼ teaspoon pepper
3 teaspoons grated onion
1 pound ground beef
2 tablespoons shortening
1 can (10¾ ounces) condensed
   cream of mushroom soup
¾ cup milk

Rinse frozen vegetables under running cold water to separate; drain. Mix egg, milk, bread crumbs, salt, mustard, celery salt, nutmeg, pepper, onion and ground beef. Shape into about 1½-inch balls. Heat shortening in 10-inch skillet until melted. Cook meatballs in shortening until done; drain.

OVEN METHOD: Place meatballs in ungreased 1½-quart casserole or 10x6x1½-inch baking dish. Mix vegetables, soup and milk. Pour over meatballs; stir. Cover and cook in 350° oven until vegetables are tender, 25 to 30 minutes.

RANGE-TOP METHOD: Remove meatballs from skillet. Mix vegetables, soup and milk in skillet. Heat to boiling; reduce heat. Cover and simmer until vegetables are tender, 10 to 15 minutes. Add meatballs; heat through.

6 servings.

*Other frozen vegetables, such as peas, beans or peas-and-carrots mixture, can be substituted for the frozen mixed vegetables.

■ **To Microwave:** Place meatballs in 8x8x2-inch microwaveproof baking dish. Cover loosely and microwave on high (100%) 4 minutes; rearrange meatballs. Cover and microwave 4 minutes; drain. Mix vegetables, soup and milk; pour over meatballs. Cover tightly and microwave until meatballs are done and vegetables are tender, 5 to 8 minutes longer.

A soup-based sauce is the meld for Meatballs with Mixed Vegetables.

WINTER BEEF STEW

2 pounds beef boneless chuck, tip or round, cut into 1-inch cubes
4 medium carrots, sliced (about 2 cups)
2 medium stalks celery, sliced (about 1 cup)
2 medium onions, sliced
1 can (8 ounces) water chestnuts, drained and sliced
1 can (4 ounces) mushroom stems and pieces, drained
3 tablespoons all-purpose flour
1 tablespoon sugar
1 tablespoon salt
1 can (16 ounces) whole tomatoes
1 cup dry red wine or beef broth

Mix beef, carrots, celery, onions, water chestnuts and mushrooms in 4-quart Dutch oven. Mix flour, sugar and salt; stir into beef mixture. Stir in tomatoes (with liquid) and the wine. Cover and cook in 325° oven until beef is tender, about 4 hours.

8 servings.

BEEF BURGUNDY

2½ pounds beef boneless chuck, tip or round (1 to 1¼ inches thick)
¼ cup vegetable oil
3 tablespoons all-purpose flour
2 teaspoons salt
2 teaspoons instant beef bouillon
¼ teaspoon dried marjoram leaves
¼ teaspoon dried thyme leaves
⅛ teaspoon pepper
1¼ cups red Burgundy or other dry red wine
¾ cup water
5 medium onions, sliced, or 12 small whole onions
8 ounces mushrooms, cut into halves
Snipped parsley

Cut beef lengthwise into ¼-inch strips; cut strips into 2- to 3-inch pieces. (For easier cutting, partially freeze beef.) Cook and stir beef in oil in 4-quart Dutch oven over medium heat until brown; drain. Sprinkle beef with flour,

salt, bouillon, marjoram, thyme and pepper. Stir in Burgundy, water and onions.

OVEN METHOD: Cover and cook in 325° oven until beef is tender, about 1½ hours. Stir in mushrooms. Cover and cook until mushrooms are done, 10 to 15 minutes. Sprinkle with parsley.

RANGE-TOP METHOD: Heat to boiling; reduce heat. Cover and simmer until beef is tender, about 1 hour. Stir in mushrooms. Cover and simmer until mushrooms are done, 10 to 15 minutes. Sprinkle with parsley.

8 to 10 servings.

BEEF BARLEY CASSEROLE

1 pound beef boneless round steak (about ½ inch thick), cut into ¾-inch pieces
1 tablespoon vegetable oil
2¾ cups water
1 can (16 ounces) whole tomatoes
2 medium carrots, chopped (about 1 cup)
2 medium onions, chopped (about 1 cup)
1 medium stalk celery, chopped
1 cup uncooked barley
2 teaspoons salt
1 teaspoon instant beef bouillon
¼ teaspoon pepper

Cook and stir beef in oil in 4-quart Dutch oven until brown; drain.

OVEN METHOD: Add water and tomatoes (with liquid); break up tomatoes with fork. Heat to boiling. Pour into ungreased 3-quart casserole or 13x9x2-inch baking dish. Stir in remaining ingredients. Cover and cook in 350° oven until beef and barley are tender, 1½ to 2 hours.

RANGE-TOP METHOD: Increase water to 3 cups. Stir in water, tomatoes (with liquid) and the remaining ingredients; break up tomatoes with fork. Heat to boiling; reduce heat. Cover and simmer, stirring occasionally, until beef and barley are tender, 1 to 1½ hours.

6 to 8 servings.

MEXICAN BEEF AND BEANS

2 tablespoons vegetable oil
2 tablespoons all-purpose flour
½ teaspoon salt
¼ teaspoon pepper
¼ teaspoon ground cumin
1 pound beef boneless chuck, tip or round, cut into 1-inch cubes
3 medium stalks celery, diagonally sliced (about 1½ cups)
2 carrots, diagonally sliced
1 large onion, coarsely chopped (about 1 cup)
½ cup water
½ cup chili sauce
1 medium green pepper, cut into ¼-inch strips
1 can (15½ ounces) kidney beans, drained

Heat oil in 10-inch skillet over medium heat until hot. Mix flour, salt, pepper and cumin; coat beef. Cook and stir beef in hot oil until brown.

OVEN METHOD: Place beef, celery, carrots and onion in ungreased 2-quart casserole or 9x9x2-inch pan. Stir in water and chili sauce. Cover and cook in 325° oven until beef is tender, 2½ to 3 hours. Stir in green pepper and beans. Cover and cook until green pepper is crisp-tender, about 10 minutes. Serve with hot cooked rice if desired.

RANGE-TOP METHOD: Add celery, carrots and onion. Stir in water and chili sauce. Heat to boiling; reduce heat. Cover and simmer, stirring occasionally, until beef is tender, 1½ to 2 hours. (Add small amount water if necessary). Stir in green pepper and beans. Cover and simmer until green pepper is crisp-tender, about 10 minutes. Serve with hot cooked rice if desired.

4 servings.

BEEF CANTONESE

2 pounds beef boneless chuck, tip or round, cut into 1-inch cubes
1 small onion, chopped
3 tablespoons shortening
1½ cups water
1 can (11 ounces) mandarin orange segments, drained (reserve syrup)
⅓ cup soy sauce
½ teaspoon ground ginger
2 tablespoons cornstarch
¼ cup cold water
1 small green pepper, cut into strips
8 ounces mushrooms, sliced
4 medium stalks celery, cut diagonally into ½-inch pieces
1 can (8 ounces) water chestnuts, drained and sliced

Cook and stir beef and onion in shortening in 10-inch skillet over medium heat until onion is tender; drain. Add 1½ cups water, the reserved orange syrup, soy sauce and ginger.

OVEN METHOD: Pour into ungreased 3-quart casserole or 13x9x2-inch baking dish. Cover and cook in 325° oven until beef is tender, 1¾ to 2 hours. Mix cornstarch and ¼ cup water; stir into beef mixture. Stir in green pepper, mushrooms, celery and water chestnuts. Cover and cook until celery is crisp-tender, 10 to 15 minutes. Fold in orange segments just before serving.

RANGE-TOP METHOD: Heat to boiling; reduce heat. Cover and simmer until beef is tender, about 1½ hours. Mix cornstarch and ¼ cup water; stir into beef mixture. Heat to boiling over medium heat, stirring constantly. Boil and stir 1 minute; reduce heat. Stir in green pepper, mushrooms, celery and water chestnuts. Cover and cook until celery is crisp-tender, 5 to 7 minutes. Fold in orange segments just before serving.

6 servings.

Pictured at right: Beef Cantonese (above)—the perfect choice for a Saturday-night dinner party.

BEEF-POTATO SCALLOP

2 pounds beef for stew, cut into
    1-inch cubes
2 large onions, sliced
2 tablespoons shortening
1 cup water
2 large potatoes, thinly sliced
1 can (10¾ ounces) condensed
    cream of mushroom soup
1 cup dairy sour cream
1¼ cups milk
1 teaspoon salt
¼ teaspoon pepper
1 cup shredded Cheddar cheese
    (about 4 ounces)
1¼ cups whole wheat flake cereal,
    crushed

Cook and stir beef and onions in shortening in 10-inch skillet until beef is brown and onions are tender. Add water. Heat to boiling; reduce heat. Cover and simmer 50 minutes.

Pour into ungreased 13x9x2-inch baking dish. Arrange potato slices on beef mixture. Mix soup, sour cream, milk, salt and pepper. Pour evenly over potatoes. Sprinkle with cheese and cereal. Cook uncovered in 350° oven until beef is tender, about 1½ hours.

8 servings.

OVEN STEW

2 pounds beef boneless round steak
    or beef for stew, cut into 1-inch
    cubes
6 medium carrots, cut into halves
6 medium potatoes, cut into halves
6 small onions
1 can (10¾ ounces) condensed
    cream of mushroom soup
1 package (about 1 ounce) brown
    gravy mix
¼ cup water
1 teaspoon prepared horseradish
½ teaspoon salt
    Cheese-Mayonnaise Biscuits
    (right)

Mix beef and vegetables in ungreased 13x9x2-inch pan. Mix soup, gravy mix, water, horseradish and salt; pour over beef mixture. Cover and cook in 325° oven until beef is tender, about 3 hours.

Increase oven temperature to 450°. Prepare Cheese-Mayonnaise Biscuits dough. Drop by spoonfuls onto hot stew. Cook uncovered until biscuits are golden brown, about 10 minutes.

6 to 8 servings.

CHEESE-MAYONNAISE BISCUITS

1 cup buttermilk baking mix
½ cup grated American cheese food
¼ cup cold water
2 tablespoons mayonnaise or salad
    dressing

Mix all ingredients until soft dough forms; beat vigorously 20 strokes.

BEEF WITH BEANS AND RICE

1 pound beef boneless round steak
    (½ inch thick), cut into 1-inch
    pieces
2 tablespoons vegetable oil
1 cup water
1 bay leaf
1 teaspoon salt
⅛ to ¼ teaspoon crushed red pepper
1 can (16 ounces) kidney beans,
    drained
1 cup uncooked regular rice
2 medium green peppers, cut into
    1-inch pieces
1 medium onion, chopped
1½ teaspoons salt
½ to 1 teaspoon curry powder
¼ teaspoon pepper

Cook and stir beef in oil in 10-inch skillet over medium heat until brown, about 15 minutes. Add water, bay leaf, 1 teaspoon salt and the red pepper. Heat to boiling; reduce heat. Cover and simmer 45 minutes.

Drain beef, reserving broth. Add enough water to broth to measure 2 cups. Mix beef, broth and remaining ingredients. Pour into ungreased 2-quart casserole. Cover and cook in 350° oven until liquid is absorbed, 45 to 50 minutes.

6 servings.

BEEF AND VEGETABLE CASSEROLE

1 pound beef boneless round steak, ½ inch thick
1 tablespoon vegetable oil
½ cup uncooked regular rice
1 can (16 ounces) whole tomatoes
1 can (4 ounces) mushroom stems and pieces
2 teaspoons salt
1 teaspoon dried basil leaves
½ teaspoon dried thyme leaves
¼ teaspoon pepper
1 can (16 ounces) cut green beans, drained
4 medium carrots, sliced (about 2 cups)
2 medium onions, sliced
1 cup shredded Cheddar or process American cheese (about 4 ounces)

Cut beef into ¼-inch strips; cut each strip into 1½- to 2-inch lengths. (For easier cutting, partially freeze beef.) Cook and stir beef in oil until beef is brown; drain.

OVEN METHOD: Mix rice, tomatoes (with liquid), mushrooms (with liquid) and seasonings in ungreased 3-quart casserole or 13x9x2-inch baking dish; break up tomatoes with fork. Add beef, beans, carrots and onions. Cover and cook in 350° oven until beef is tender and rice is done, 1 to 1¼ hours. Sprinkle with cheese. Cook uncovered until cheese is melted, 3 to 5 minutes.

RANGE-TOP METHOD: Drain beans, reserving ½ cup liquid. Place beef, tomatoes (with liquid), mushrooms (with liquid), seasonings, beans, reserved bean liquid, the carrots and onions in 4-quart Dutch oven; break up tomatoes with fork. Heat to boiling; reduce heat. Cover and simmer until beef is almost tender, about 45 minutes. Stir in rice. Cover and simmer, stirring occasionally, until rice is done, 20 to 25 minutes. Sprinkle with cheese. Cover and let stand until cheese is melted, 3 to 5 minutes.

6 servings.

STEAK AND KIDNEY PIE

1 pound beef round steak
1 beef kidney
¼ cup all-purpose flour
1 teaspoon salt
⅛ teaspoon pepper
3 tablespoons shortening
1 medium onion, chopped
¼ cup chopped pimiento
2 tablespoons Worcestershire sauce
¼ teaspoon ground thyme
1¼ cups water
Potato Pastry (below)

Cut steak and kidney into 1-inch pieces. Mix flour, salt and pepper; coat meat, reserving remaining flour mixture. Heat shortening in 10-inch skillet until melted. Cook and stir meat and onion until onion is tender. Stir in pimiento, Worcestershire sauce, thyme and water. Cover and simmer until meat is tender, 45 minutes.

Prepare Potato Pastry. Moisten rim of 9x1¼-inch pie plate; press pastry strip onto rim. Add reserved flour mixture to meat mixture. Heat to boiling, stirring constantly. Boil and stir 1 minute. Pour into pie plate. Moisten edge of pastry on rim. Cover filling with pastry circle; seal and flute. Cook in 325° oven until crust is brown, about 45 minutes.

6 servings.

POTATO PASTRY

Instant mashed potatoes for 2 servings
1½ cups all-purpose flour
2 teaspoons baking powder
½ teaspoon salt
⅓ cup shortening
¼ cup milk or water

Prepare mashed potatoes as directed on package; cool. Mix flour, baking powder and salt. Cut in potatoes and shortening thoroughly. Stir in milk. Gather dough into a ball; shape into flattened round on floured cloth-covered board. Roll dough into 11-inch circle. Cut a 1-inch-wide strip from edge; reserve. Cut large slits in remaining pastry circle.

BEEF-SAUSAGE ROLLS

6 ounces bulk pork sausage
½ cup soft bread crumbs (about 1 slice bread)
1 small stalk celery, chopped (about ¼ cup)
2 tablespoons finely chopped onion
⅛ teaspoon ground sage
⅛ teaspoon dried thyme leaves
4 beef cubed steaks (about 3 ounces each)
1 can (10¾ ounces) condensed cream of mushroom soup
¼ cup water
1 can (16 ounces) French-style green beans, drained

Cook and stir pork in 10-inch skillet over medium heat until brown; drain. Mix bread crumbs, celery, onion, sage and thyme. Stir in pork. Press about ¼ cup pork mixture evenly onto each beef steak. Roll up, beginning at short side; secure with wooden picks. Cook meat rolls in same skillet over medium heat until brown (add 1 tablespoon vegetable oil if necessary).

OVEN METHOD: Place meat rolls in ungreased 1½-quart casserole or 10x6x1½-inch baking dish. Mix soup and water; pour into casserole around meat rolls. Cover and cook in 350° oven until tender, about 45 minutes. Stir in beans. Cover and cook until beans are hot, about 10 minutes. Serve gravy over meat rolls.

RANGE-TOP METHOD: Mix soup and water; pour into skillet around meat rolls. Heat to boiling; reduce heat. Cover and simmer until meat is tender, about 45 minutes. Add beans. Cover and cook until beans are hot, about 10 minutes. Serve gravy over meat rolls.

4 servings.

Do-ahead Note: Prepare as directed for Oven Method except—after pouring soup mixture around meat rolls, cover and refrigerate no longer than 24 hours. To serve, cover and cook in 350° oven about 1¼ hours.

BEEF HASH

2 cups cut-up cooked beef
2 cups chopped cooked potatoes
⅔ cup chopped onion
2 tablespoons snipped parsley
½ teaspoon salt
⅛ teaspoon pepper
¼ cup water

Mix beef, potatoes, onion, parsley, salt and pepper.

OVEN METHOD: Spread beef mixture in greased 2-quart casserole or 8x8x2-inch baking dish. Sprinkle water over top. Cook uncovered in 350° oven 20 minutes.

RANGE-TOP METHOD: Heat ¼ cup shortening in 10-inch skillet over medium heat until melted. Spread beef mixture in skillet. Cook, turning frequently with wide spatula, until brown, 10 to 15 minutes; reduce heat. Stir in ⅔ cup water. Cover and cook until crisp, about 10 minutes longer.

4 servings.

Corned Beef Hash: Prepare as directed for Range-top Method except—substitute 1 can (12 ounces) corned beef, chopped, for the cooked beef. Add ¼ teaspoon garlic powder with the salt and omit water. Do not cook hash after browning.

■ **To Microwave:** Spread beef mixture in 1-quart microwaveproof casserole. Sprinkle water over top. Cover tightly and microwave on high (100%) 5 minutes; stir. Cover and microwave until hot, 3 to 5 minutes longer. If desired, set oven control to broil and/or 550°; broil with top about 3 inches from heat just until light brown, about 1 minute.

BEEF SLICES WITH VEGETABLES

3 carrots, cut into 3x⅜-inch strips
2 parsnips, cut into 3x⅜-inch strips
8 slices cooked beef
1 cup beef gravy
2 cups seasoned mashed potatoes
1 tablespoon instant minced onion
1 tablespoon snipped chives
2 teaspoons prepared mustard
2 tablespoons grated Parmesan
   cheese

Heat 1 inch salted water (½ teaspoon salt to 1 cup water) to boiling. Add carrots and parsnips. Cook uncovered until tender, 18 to 20 minutes; drain. Overlap beef slices in ungreased 2-quart casserole or 8x8x2-inch baking dish. Pour gravy over beef. Mix potatoes, onion, chives and mustard. Drop by spoonfuls around edge of casserole. Arrange carrots and parsnips in center; sprinkle with cheese. Cook uncovered in 350° oven until gravy is hot and bubbly, about 30 minutes.

4 to 6 servings.

CORNED BEEF 'N NOODLE CASSEROLE

1 can (10¾ ounces) condensed
   cream of chicken soup
1 cup milk
1 can (12 ounces) corned beef (about
   1½ cups)
1 cup shredded Cheddar cheese
   (about 4 ounces)
1 medium onion, finely chopped
   (about ½ cup)
¼ teaspoon pepper
4 cups uncooked egg noodles (about
   8 ounces)
½ cup dry bread crumbs
1 tablespoon margarine or butter,
   melted

Mix soup, milk, corned beef, cheese, onion and pepper. Spread half of the corned beef mixture in greased 2-quart casserole or 12x7½x2-inch baking dish. Top with noodles and remaining corned beef mixture. Mix bread crumbs and margarine; sprinkle over noodles. Cook uncovered in 375° oven until hot and bubbly and noodles are tender, 40 to 45 minutes.

6 to 8 servings.

■ **To Microwave:** Layer corned beef mixture and noodles in 2-quart microwaveproof casserole as directed. Cover tightly and microwave on high (100%) 8 minutes; sprinkle with buttered bread crumbs. Microwave uncovered until hot and bubbly and noodles are tender, 4 to 6 minutes longer.

DRIED BEEF CASSEROLE

1 cup uncooked elbow macaroni
1 can (10¾ ounces) condensed
   cream of mushroom soup
½ cup milk
1 cup shredded Cheddar or process
   American cheese (about 4
   ounces)
3 tablespoons finely chopped onion
1 jar (2½ ounces) dried beef, cut
   into bite-size pieces
2 hard-cooked eggs, sliced

Cook macaroni as directed on package; drain. Mix soup and milk. Stir in cheese, onion, beef and macaroni; fold in eggs.

OVEN METHOD: Pour into ungreased 1½-quart casserole or 10x6x1½-inch baking dish. Cover and cook in 350° oven until hot and bubbly, about 30 minutes.

RANGE-TOP METHOD: Pour into 2-quart saucepan. Heat to boiling; reduce heat. Cover and simmer, stirring occasionally, until hot and bubbly, 8 to 10 minutes.

4 to 6 servings.

■ **To Microwave:** Place uncooked macaroni and 1 cup water in 2-quart microwaveproof casserole. Cover tightly and microwave on high (100%) to boiling, 4 to 5 minutes. Let stand 5 minutes. Mix soup and ⅓ cup milk. Stir in cheese, onion and beef; fold in eggs. Stir into macaroni. Cover tightly and microwave 4 minutes; stir. Cover and microwave until hot and bubbly, 3 to 5 minutes longer.

BEEF AND CORN CASSEROLE

½ small green pepper, chopped
    (about ¼ cup)
1 small onion, chopped (about ¼
    cup)
1 tablespoon margarine or butter
2 packages (2½ ounces each) thinly
    sliced smoked beef, chopped
1 cup sliced mushrooms
¼ cup margarine or butter
¼ cup all-purpose flour
½ teaspoon salt
¼ teaspoon pepper
2 cups milk
2 egg yolks, slightly beaten
1 teaspoon prepared mustard
1 can (17 ounces) whole kernel corn,
    drained
⅓ cup dry bread crumbs
¼ cup grated Parmesan cheese
2 tablespoons margarine or butter,
    melted
¼ teaspoon paprika

Cook and stir green pepper and onion in 1 tablespoon margarine in 10-inch skillet until onion is tender. Add beef and mushrooms; cook and stir until edges of beef curl.

Heat ¼ cup margarine in 1-quart saucepan over low heat until melted. Stir in flour, salt and pepper. Cook, stirring constantly, until smooth and bubbly; remove from heat. Stir in milk. Heat to boiling, stirring constantly. Boil and stir 1 minute. Stir at least half of the hot mixture gradually into egg yolks. Blend into hot mixture in saucepan. Boil and stir 1 minute; stir in mustard. Stir sauce and corn into beef mixture.

OVEN METHOD: Pour into ungreased 1½-quart casserole or 10x6x1½-inch baking dish. Mix remaining ingredients; sprinkle over beef mixture. Cook uncovered in 350° oven until hot and bubbly, about 30 minutes.

RANGE-TOP METHOD: Heat to boiling; reduce heat. Simmer uncovered, stirring occasionally, until hot, 5 to 8 minutes; remove from heat. Mix remaining ingredients; sprinkle over beef mixture.

6 servings.

BEEF LIVER CASSEROLE

4 slices bacon
4 green onions (with tops), sliced
2 tablespoons all-purpose flour
1 tablespoon chili powder
1 pound beef liver, cut into ¼-inch
    strips
1 can (16 ounces) whole tomatoes
1 can (15½ ounces) kidney beans,
    drained
1 teaspoon salt
    Dash of pepper
1 hard-cooked egg, chopped

Fry bacon in 12-inch skillet until crisp; drain and crumble. Drain fat, reserving 2 tablespoons in skillet. Cook and stir onions in fat in skillet until tender, about 1 minute.

Mix flour and chili powder. Coat liver with flour mixture; add to onions in skillet. Cook and stir over medium heat until liver is light brown. Mix liver, onions, tomatoes (with liquid), beans, salt and pepper in ungreased 2-quart casserole or 12x7½x2-inch baking dish. Cook uncovered in 350° oven until liver is done, 25 to 30 minutes. Sprinkle with bacon and the egg.

4 servings.

Fresh Out?

When a recipe calls for a fresh seasoning, but you're fresh out, you can rely on dry and instant forms to come to the rescue:

Garlic: ¼ teaspoon instant minced garlic or ⅛ teaspoon garlic powder equals 1 clove

Chopped onion: 2 tablespoons instant minced onion or onion flakes or 1 teaspoon onion powder equals ½ cup

Herbs: 1 teaspoon dried herbs or ¼ teaspoon ground herbs equals 1 tablespoon snipped fresh

---

BEER STEW

1 pound pork shoulder roll or smoked hocks, cut into 1-inch pieces
1 pound beef boneless chuck, tip or round, cut into 1-inch pieces
3 tablespoons vegetable oil
1 can or bottle (12 ounces) beer
1 tablespoon instant beef bouillon
1½ teaspoons salt
½ teaspoon garlic salt
⅛ teaspoon ground marjoram
⅛ teaspoon ground thyme
⅛ teaspoon dried basil leaves
6 medium carrots, cut into 1-inch pieces
3 medium potatoes, cut into 1-inch pieces
1 medium onion, thinly sliced
½ cup cold water
¼ cup all-purpose flour
¾ cup walnut halves (optional)
1 tablespoon margarine or butter, melted (optional)

Cook and stir pork and beef in oil in 4-quart Dutch oven over medium heat until beef is brown, about 8 minutes; drain. Add enough water to beer to measure 2 cups; pour over meat. Add bouillon and seasonings. Heat to boiling; reduce heat. Add carrots, potatoes and onion.

OVEN METHOD: Cover and cook in 325° oven until meat is tender, about 1½ hours; remove from oven. Shake ½ cup cold water and the flour in tightly covered container; stir into stew. Cover and cook in oven 10 minutes. Mix walnuts and margarine; sprinkle over stew.

RANGE-TOP METHOD: Cover and simmer until meat is tender, about 1½ hours. Shake ½ cup cold water and the flour in tightly covered container; stir into stew. Heat to boiling, stirring constantly. Boil and stir 1 minute. Mix walnuts and margarine; sprinkle over stew.

8 servings.

Note: The beef in this recipe will assume a pink color because of the smoked pork.

PORK CHOP AND POTATO CASSEROLE

6 pork loin or rib chops, ½ inch thick
2 tablespoons vegetable oil
1 can (10¾ ounces) condensed cream of mushroom soup
1 can (4 ounces) mushroom stems and pieces
¼ cup water
½ teaspoon garlic salt
¼ teaspoon dried thyme leaves
2 tablespoons dry white wine
½ teaspoon Worcestershire sauce
1 tablespoon chopped pimiento
1 can (16 ounces) whole potatoes, drained
1 package (10 ounces) frozen green peas, rinsed and drained

Cook pork in oil in 10-inch skillet over medium-high heat until brown on both sides.

OVEN METHOD: Place pork in ungreased 13x9x2-inch pan. Mix soup, mushrooms (with liquid), water, garlic salt, thyme, wine and Worcestershire sauce; pour over pork. Cover and cook in 350° oven 1 hour. Stir in pimiento, potatoes and peas. Cover and cook until peas are tender and potatoes are hot, about 15 minutes.

RANGE-TOP METHOD: Mix soup, mushrooms (with liquid), water, garlic salt, thyme, wine and Worcestershire sauce; pour over pork. Heat to boiling, stirring occasionally; reduce heat. Cover and simmer 30 minutes. Stir in pimiento, potatoes and peas. Cover and simmer, stirring occasionally, until peas are tender and potatoes are hot, about 10 minutes.

6 servings.

PORK CHOPS
WITH FRUITED RICE

1 can (16 ounces) sliced peaches,
    drained (reserve syrup)
¾ cup uncooked regular rice
1 tablespoon margarine or butter
1 teaspoon salt
1 teaspoon ground sage
½ teaspoon ground cloves
4 pork loin or rib chops, about
    ½ inch thick
  Salt and pepper
1 cup pitted prunes

Add enough boiling water to reserved peach syrup to measure 2 cups. Mix syrup mixture, rice, margarine, 1 teaspoon salt, the sage and cloves in ungreased 2-quart casserole or 12x7½x2-inch baking dish. Trim excess fat from pork. Arrange pork on rice; sprinkle with salt and pepper. Arrange prunes on pork. Cover and cook in 350° oven 1 hour. Add peaches; cook uncovered until pork is brown, about 15 minutes.

4 servings.

CHINESE PORK AND RICE

⅔ cup uncooked regular rice
1 medium onion, chopped (about
    ½ cup)
2 tablespoons vegetable oil
2 cups cut-up cooked pork (¾- to
    1-inch pieces)
1½ cups boiling water
2 tablespoons soy sauce
1 teaspoon instant chicken or beef
    bouillon
2 medium stalks celery, diagonally
    sliced (about 1 cup)
1 medium green pepper, chopped
    (about 1 cup)

Cook and stir rice and onion in oil in 10-inch skillet over medium heat until rice is golden brown. Stir in pork, water, soy sauce and bouillon. Pour into ungreased 2-quart casserole or 12x7½x2-inch baking dish. Cover and cook in 375° oven 35 minutes. Stir in celery and green pepper. Cover and cook until rice is tender and liquid is absorbed, about 10 minutes longer. Sprinkle with cashews if desired.

4 servings.

Pork Chops with Fruited Rice—simply add a vegetable and dinner's complete.

PORK 'N NOODLE CASSEROLE

2 cups cut-up cooked pork
2 tablespoons vegetable oil
2 cups uncooked egg noodles
2 cups water
1 can (10 ¾ ounces) condensed
    cream of chicken soup
1 can (8 ounces) whole kernel corn,
    drained
1 jar (2 ounces) diced pimiento,
    drained
1 cup shredded sharp Cheddar
    cheese (about 4 ounces)
1 small green pepper, chopped
    (about ½ cup)

Cook and stir pork in oil in 10-inch skillet over medium-high heat until brown; drain. Stir in remaining ingredients.

OVEN METHOD: Pour into ungreased 2-quart casserole or 12x7½x2-inch baking dish. Cook uncovered in 375° oven until noodles are tender, about 45 minutes.

RANGE-TOP METHOD: Heat to boiling; reduce heat. Simmer uncovered, stirring occasionally, until noodles are tender, about 20 minutes.

6 servings.

■ **To Microwave:** Omit oil. Decrease water to 1½ cups. Mix all ingredients in 2-quart microwaveproof casserole. Cover tightly and microwave on high (100%) 10 minutes; stir. Cover and microwave until noodles are tender, 8 to 11 minutes longer. Let stand 5 minutes.

PORK 'N SWEET POTATO CASSEROLE

1 can (12 ounces) pork luncheon
    meat
1 can (17 ounces) vacuum-pack
    whole sweet potatoes
½ cup corn syrup
¼ cup crunchy peanut butter
1 can (8¼ ounces) pineapple chunks,
    drained (reserve syrup)
1 tablespoon margarine or butter,
    melted

Cut luncheon meat into 4 slices; place in ungreased 9x9x2-inch pan. Arrange sweet potatoes on top. Mix corn syrup and peanut butter; stir in reserved pineapple syrup and the margarine. Pour over meat and sweet potatoes. Top with pineapple. Cook uncovered in 375° oven until hot and bubbly, 25 to 30 minutes.

4 servings.

■ **To Microwave:** Place slices of luncheon meat in 10x6x1½-inch microwaveproof baking dish. Continue as directed. Cover tightly and microwave on high (100%) 5 minutes; rotate dish ½ turn. Microwave until hot, 4 to 6 minutes longer.

HAM AND EGGPLANT AU GRATIN

¼ cup margarine or butter
¼ cup all-purpose flour
1 teaspoon dry mustard
½ teaspoon salt
¼ teaspoon pepper
¼ teaspoon paprika
2 cups milk
1 jar (5 ounces) pimiento cheese
 spread
1 small onion, chopped (about ¼ cup)
1 medium eggplant, cut into ½-inch
 cubes
2 cups cut-up fully cooked smoked
 ham
2 medium tomatoes, cut into
 ½-inch slices
½ cup whole wheat flake cereal,
 slightly crushed
¼ cup margarine or butter, melted

Heat ¼ cup margarine in 2-quart saucepan over low heat until melted. Stir in flour, mustard, salt, pepper and paprika. Cook, stirring constantly, until smooth and bubbly; remove from heat. Stir in milk. Heat to boiling, stirring constantly. Boil and stir 1 minute. Stir in cheese spread and onion. Heat over low heat, stirring occasionally, until cheese is melted.

Layer half each of the eggplant, ham and cheese sauce in ungreased 12x7½x2-inch baking dish; repeat. Top with tomatoes. Mix cereal and ¼ cup margarine; sprinkle over tomatoes. Cook uncovered in 350° oven until hot and bubbly, 25 to 30 minutes.

6 to 8 servings.

HAM POPOVER

1 package (10 ounces) frozen cut
 asparagus
¼ cup margarine or butter
¼ cup all-purpose flour
½ teaspoon salt
½ teaspoon ground nutmeg
¼ teaspoon pepper
2¼ cups milk
2 cups cut-up fully cooked smoked
 ham
1 teaspoon lemon juice
1 teaspoon Dijon-style mustard
2 cups shredded Swiss cheese
 (about 8 ounces)
2 eggs
1 cup milk
1 tablespoon vegetable oil
1 cup all-purpose flour
½ teaspoon salt
½ cup sliced almonds
2 green onions (with tops), sliced

Rinse frozen asparagus under running cold water to separate; drain. Heat margarine over low heat until melted. Stir in ¼ cup flour, ½ teaspoon salt, the nutmeg and pepper. Cook, stirring constantly, until smooth and bubbly; remove from heat. Stir in 2¼ cups milk. Heat to boiling, stirring constantly. Boil and stir 1 minute. Stir in asparagus, ham, lemon juice and mustard. Pour into ungreased 13x9x2-inch pan. Sprinkle with cheese.

Beat eggs, 1 cup milk, the oil, 1 cup flour and ½ teaspoon salt with hand beater until smooth; pour over cheese. Sprinkle with almonds and onions. Cook uncovered in 425° oven until puffy and golden brown, 25 to 30 minutes.

8 servings.

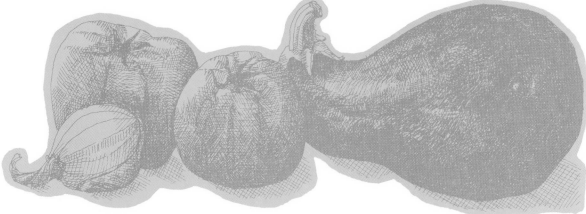

LAYERED HAM DINNER

1 package (9 ounces) frozen cut
    green beans
1 can (10¾ ounces) condensed
    cream of celery soup
¼ cup mayonnaise or salad dressing
1 tablespoon prepared mustard
2 packages (2½ ounces each) thinly
    sliced smoked ham or 6 ounces
    fully cooked smoked ham, cut
    into ¼-inch strips
1 cup shredded process American
    or Cheddar cheese (about 4
    ounces)
¼ cup dry bread crumbs

Rinse frozen beans under running cold water to separate; drain. Place beans in ungreased 1½-quart casserole or 10x6x1½-inch baking dish. Mix soup, mayonnaise and mustard; spoon half of the mixture onto beans. Top with ham; spoon remaining soup mixture onto ham. Sprinkle with cheese and bread crumbs. Cook uncovered in 350° oven until hot and bubbly, about 20 minutes.

4 to 6 servings.

■ **To Microwave:** Place frozen beans in 1½-quart microwaveproof casserole. Cover tightly and microwave on high (100%) 3 minutes; stir. Microwave until thawed, 2 to 3 minutes longer; drain. Layer soup mixture and ham as directed. Cover tightly and microwave 6 minutes. Sprinkle with cheese and bread crumbs; rotate casserole ½ turn. Microwave uncovered until hot and bubbly, 2 to 4 minutes longer.

HAM 'N CHEESE BAKE

1 medium onion, chopped (about ½
    cup)
1 tablespoon margarine or butter
1 can (6¾ ounces) chunk ham,
    drained
1 medium tomato, chopped (about
    ¾ cup)
2 cups buttermilk baking mix
½ cup cold water
1 cup shredded Swiss or Cheddar
    cheese (about 4 ounces)
¼ cup milk
2 eggs
¼ teaspoon salt
¼ teaspoon pepper
¼ teaspoon dried dill weed (optional)
2 tablespoons snipped chives

Cook and stir onion in margarine in 10-inch skillet until tender; remove from heat. Stir in ham and tomato. Mix baking mix and water until soft dough forms; beat vigorously 20 strokes. Pat dough in lightly greased 13x9x2-inch pan with floured hands, pressing dough ½ inch up sides. Spread ham mixture over dough; sprinkle with cheese. Beat milk, eggs, salt, pepper and dill weed with hand beater until foamy; slowly pour over cheese. Sprinkle with chives. Cook uncovered in 350° oven until golden brown, 25 to 30 minutes.

6 to 8 servings.

Cutting the Cost of Cheese

Cheese is an integral part of many casseroles, adding color, flavor and protein. Here are some economical buy-lines to keep in mind when buying cheese for your recipes:

■ Domestic cheese often costs less than an imported cheese of the same type and quality.

■ Pasteurized process cheese often costs less than sharp, aged cheese.

■ Process cheese in loaf form costs less than the spreads.

■ Blocks of cheese usually cost less than sliced or shredded cheese.

HAM AND DUMPLINGS

   1 package (10 ounces) frozen baby
          lima beans, rinsed and drained
   1 cup cut-up fully cooked smoked
          ham
   3 tablespoons chopped pimiento
   2 tablespoons chopped onion
   1 can (10¾ ounces) condensed
          cream of chicken soup
1⅓ cups water
   ½ teaspoon Worcestershire sauce
   ¼ teaspoon dry mustard
   ⅛ teaspoon pepper
          Dumplings (below)
   ½ cup dry bread crumbs
   2 tablespoons margarine or butter,
          melted

OVEN METHOD: Mix beans, ham, pimiento, onion, soup, water, Worcestershire sauce, mustard and pepper in ungreased 2-quart casserole or 12x7½x2-inch baking dish. Cook uncovered in 425° oven until hot and bubbly, 20 to 25 minutes. Prepare Dumplings; drop by spoonfuls onto hot ham mixture. Mix bread crumbs and margarine; sprinkle over dumplings and ham mixture. Cook uncovered in oven until dumplings are done, 20 to 25 minutes longer.

RANGE-TOP METHOD: Mix beans, ham, pimiento, onion, soup, water, Worcestershire sauce, mustard and pepper in 10-inch skillet. Heat to boiling; reduce heat. Cover and simmer until beans are tender, 10 to 12 minutes. Prepare Dumplings; drop by spoonfuls onto hot ham mixture. Mix bread crumbs and margarine; sprinkle over dumplings and ham mixture. Cook uncovered 10 minutes. Cover and cook 10 minutes longer.

4 to 6 servings.

DUMPLINGS

   1 cup all-purpose flour
   2 teaspoons baking powder
   ¼ teaspoon salt
   ½ teaspoon celery seed
   ½ teaspoon poultry seasoning
   ½ cup milk
   2 tablespoons vegetable oil

Mix flour, baking powder, salt, celery seed and poultry seasoning in 1-quart bowl. Add milk and vegetable oil, all at once; stir just until mixture is well blended.

■ **To Microwave:** Decrease water to 1 cup. Mix ingredients as directed in 3-quart microwave-proof casserole. Cover tightly and microwave on high (100%) until hot and bubbly, 10 to 12 minutes; stir. Prepare Dumplings; drop by spoonfuls around edge of casserole. Cover tightly and microwave on medium (50%) until dumplings are no longer doughy, 7 to 10 minutes.

CANADIAN BACON AND ZUCCHINI BAKE

   2 eggs
   2 cups creamed cottage cheese
   ¾ cup uncooked instant rice
   1 medium onion, chopped (about
          ½ cup)
   2 tablespoons snipped parsley
1½ teaspoons dried marjoram leaves
   ¾ teaspoon salt
          Few drops red pepper sauce
   2 pounds zucchini, cut into
          ½-inch slices
   ¾ cup grated Parmesan cheese
   1 pound Canadian-style bacon, cut
          into 16 slices

Beat eggs slightly with fork; stir in cottage cheese, rice, onion, parsley, marjoram, salt and pepper sauce. Arrange half of the zucchini slices in ungreased 2-quart casserole or 12x7½x2-inch baking dish. Cover with half of the cheese-rice mixture. Repeat with remaining zucchini and cheese-rice mixture; sprinkle with Parmesan cheese. Overlap bacon slices on top. Cook uncovered in 350° oven until golden brown, about 1 hour.

8 servings.

Pictured at right: A trio of interesting toppings— flaky biscuits crown Chicken and Biscuits (page 52), colorful bacon slices circle Canadian Bacon and Zucchini Bake (above), tomatoes and cheese cover Chili-Zucchini Casserole (page 79).

BACON-CHEESE MACARONI

1 package (7 ounces) elbow
   macaroni
1 can (4 ounces) chopped green
   chilies, drained
2 cups shredded Cheddar cheese
   (about 8 ounces)
1 cup dairy sour cream
¼ cup finely chopped onion
½ teaspoon salt
½ teaspoon dried oregano leaves
6 slices bacon, crisply fried and
   crumbled
1 cup herb-seasoned croutons

Cook macaroni as directed on package; drain. Mix macaroni, chilies, 1½ cups of the cheese, the sour cream, onion, salt and oregano in ungreased 2-quart casserole. Mix bacon, croutons and the remaining cheese; sprinkle over macaroni. Cook uncovered in 375° oven until hot and bubbly, 25 to 30 minutes.

5 servings.

FRANK-MACARONI PIE

1 cup uncooked macaroni rings
   (3½ ounces)
½ cup creamed cottage cheese (small
   curd)
1 egg, slightly beaten
¾ teaspoon salt
   Dash of pepper
½ cup shredded sharp Cheddar
   cheese (about 2 ounces)
2 frankfurters, thinly sliced
2 medium tomatoes, sliced
1 egg
2 tablespoons grated Parmesan
   cheese
⅛ teaspoon dried oregano leaves

Cook macaroni as directed on package; drain. Mix macaroni, cottage cheese, beaten egg, salt, pepper, Cheddar cheese and frankfurter slices. Pour into greased 9x1¼-inch pie plate. Arrange tomato slices on top. Mix egg, Parmesan cheese and oregano; pour over tomatoes. Cook uncovered in 350° oven until bubbly, 25 to 30 minutes.

5 servings.

FRANKFURTER-NOODLE CASSEROLE

2 tablespoons margarine or butter
2 tablespoons all-purpose flour
½ teaspoon salt
1½ cups milk
1 cup shredded Cheddar cheese
   (about 4 ounces)
1 teaspoon prepared mustard
3 cups cooked egg noodles
4 frankfurters, cut into ½-inch
   slices
2 apples, thinly sliced
1 tablespoon packed brown sugar

Heat margarine in saucepan over low heat until melted. Stir in flour and salt. Cook over low heat, stirring constantly, until smooth and bubbly; remove from heat. Stir in milk. Heat to boiling, stirring constantly. Boil and stir 1 minute. Stir in ¾ cup of the cheese and the mustard. Cook over low heat until cheese is melted.

Mix cheese sauce, noodles, frankfurters and apples in ungreased 2-quart casserole or 12x7½x2-inch baking dish. Sprinkle with remaining cheese and the brown sugar. Cook uncovered in 350° oven until hot and bubbly, about 30 minutes.

4 servings.

ZUCCHINI AND FRANKS

1 can (28 ounces) whole tomatoes
6 frankfurters, diagonally sliced
2 small onions, thinly sliced
1 small zucchini, sliced
1 cup uncooked elbow macaroni
1½ teaspoons dried basil leaves
1 teaspoon salt
½ teaspoon garlic salt
⅛ teaspoon pepper

Mix tomatoes (with liquid) and the remaining ingredients in ungreased 2-quart casserole or 12x7½x2-inch baking dish; break up tomatoes with fork. Cook uncovered in 350° oven until macaroni is tender, 35 to 40 minutes. Serve with grated Parmesan cheese if desired.

6 servings.

SAUSAGE-BROWN RICE CASEROLE

12 ounces bulk pork sausage
2 cups cooked brown rice
⅓ cup milk
1 large stalk celery, chopped (about ¾ cup)
⅓ cup chopped green pepper
1 small onion, chopped (about ¼ cup)
1 can (10¾ ounces) condensed cream of mushroom soup
1 can (4 ounces) mushroom stems and pieces
½ cup shredded process American cheese

Cook and stir pork in 10-inch skillet until brown; drain. Stir in rice, milk, celery, green pepper, onion, soup and mushrooms (with liquid).

OVEN METHOD: Pour into ungreased 2-quart casserole or 12x7½x2-inch baking dish. Sprinkle with cheese. Cook uncovered in 350° oven until center is hot and bubbly, about 45 minutes.

RANGE-TOP METHOD: Heat to boiling; reduce heat. Cover and simmer, stirring occasionally, until celery is tender, 10 to 15 minutes. Sprinkle with cheese. Cover and let stand 5 minutes.

4 servings.

■ **To Microwave:** Crumble pork into 2-quart microwaveproof casserole. Cover loosely and microwave on high (100%) 3 minutes; break up and stir. Cover and microwave until no longer pink, 3 to 5 minutes longer; drain. Stir in remaining ingredients except cheese. Cover tightly and microwave 6 minutes; stir. Cover and microwave until hot and bubbly, 5 to 7 minutes longer. Sprinkle with cheese. Cover and let stand 5 minutes.

LASAGNE

1 pound bulk Italian sausage or ground beef
1 medium onion, chopped (about ½ cup)
1 clove garlic, pressed
1 can (16 ounces) whole tomatoes
1 can (15 ounces) tomato sauce
2 tablespoons parsley flakes
1 teaspoon sugar
1 teaspoon dried basil leaves
½ teaspoon salt
9 uncooked lasagne noodles (about 8 ounces)
2 cups ricotta or creamed cottage cheese
¼ cup grated Parmesan cheese
1 tablespoon parsley flakes
1½ teaspoons salt
1½ teaspoons dried oregano leaves
2 cups shredded mozzarella cheese (about 8 ounces)
¼ cup grated Parmesan cheese

Cook and stir sausage, onion and garlic in 10-inch skillet until sausage is brown; drain. Add tomatoes (with liquid), tomato sauce, 2 tablespoons parsley, the sugar, basil and ½ teaspoon salt. Heat to boiling, stirring occasionally; reduce heat. Simmer uncovered until consistency of thick spaghetti sauce, about 1 hour.

Cook noodles as directed on package; drain. Reserve ½ cup of the sauce mixture. Mix ricotta cheese, ¼ cup Parmesan cheese, 1 tablespoon parsley, 1½ teaspoons salt and the oregano. Layer ⅓ each of the noodles, remaining sauce mixture, mozzarella cheese and ricotta cheese mixture in ungreased 13x9x2-inch pan; repeat 2 times. Spoon reserved sauce mixture over top; sprinkle with ¼ cup Parmesan cheese. Cook uncovered in 350° oven until hot and bubbly, about 45 minutes. Let stand 15 minutes before cutting.

8 to 10 servings.

Do-ahead Note: Before cooking, cover and refrigerate no longer than 24 hours. To serve, cook uncovered in 350° oven 55 to 60 minutes. Or, after cooking, wrap, label and freeze no longer than 3 weeks. To serve, cook uncovered in 375° oven about 1 hour.

SAUSAGE AND VEGETABLE POPOVER

4 precooked Polish sausages (about 1 pound), sliced
1 can (4 ounces) chopped green chilies, drained
1½ teaspoons chili powder
1 teaspoon dried oregano leaves
1 teaspoon seasoned salt
½ teaspoon ground cumin
½ teaspoon garlic salt
½ teaspoon sugar
1 tablespoon vegetable oil
1 can (12 ounces) whole kernel corn with sweet peppers, drained
1 can (4 ounces) mushroom stems and pieces, drained
1 tablespoon margarine or butter
2 eggs
¾ cup all-purpose flour
¾ cup milk
1 cup shredded Monterey Jack or Cheddar cheese (about 4 ounces)
2 green onions (with tops), chopped

Cook and stir sausages, chilies, chili powder, oregano, seasoned salt, cumin, garlic salt and sugar in oil in 12-inch skillet until sausages are light brown. Stir in corn and mushrooms; keep warm.

Heat oven to 400°. Heat margarine in 9x1¼-inch pie plate in oven until melted. Beat eggs, flour and milk until smooth; pour into pie plate. Mound sausage mixture in pie plate to within 1 inch of edge. Cook uncovered 20 minutes; sprinkle with cheese. Cook until cheese is melted, 10 to 15 minutes. Sprinkle with onions.

4 servings.

Pictured at left: Sausage and Vegetable Popover (above)—just add a tossed green salad for dinnertime simplicity.

SAUSAGE AND SAUERKRAUT

2 apples, each cut into 16 wedges
2 medium onions, coarsely chopped (about 1 cup)
1 can (27 ounces) sauerkraut, drained
1 cup dry white wine
1 tablespoon packed brown sugar
8 ounces smoked thuringer, cut into 10 pieces
3 links fresh bratwurst
3 small links smoked pork sausage
Paprika

Mix apples, onions, sauerkraut, wine and brown sugar in ungreased 3-quart casserole or 13x9x2-inch baking dish; place meat on top. Cover tightly and cook in 350° oven 30 minutes. Uncover and cook until bratwurst are done, 35 to 45 minutes longer. Sprinkle with paprika.

6 servings.

SPICY PIZZA BAKE

1 pound bulk Italian sausage
1 medium onion, chopped (about ½ cup)
¼ cup chopped green pepper
1 can (15 ounces) tomato sauce
½ cup sliced ripe olives
2 tablespoons buttermilk baking mix
2 cups shredded mozzarella cheese (about 8 ounces)
1 cup buttermilk baking mix
1 cup milk
2 eggs
¼ cup grated Parmesan cheese

Heat oven to 425°. Cook and stir sausage, onion and green pepper in 10-inch skillet until sausage is brown; drain. Stir in tomato sauce, olives and 2 tablespoons baking mix. Heat to boiling, stirring frequently. Boil and stir 1 minute. Pour into ungreased 13x9x2-inch pan; sprinkle with mozzarella cheese. Beat 1 cup baking mix, the milk and eggs until smooth; pour over mozzarella cheese. Sprinkle with Parmesan cheese. Cook uncovered until topping is golden, about 20 minutes.

6 servings.

BOLOGNA-NOODLE-BEAN BAKE

4 cups uncooked egg noodles (about 8 ounces)
1-pound ring bologna (casing removed)
1 large onion, chopped (about 1 cup)
2 medium stalks celery, chopped (about 1 cup)
1 small green pepper, cut into strips
1 tablespoon vegetable oil
1 can (8 ounces) tomato sauce
2 to 3 teaspoons chili powder
1 can (15 ounces) garbanzo beans or kidney beans
½ cup sliced pitted ripe olives
1 can (16 ounces) whole kernel corn
1 can (11 ounces) condensed Cheddar cheese soup
2 cups whole wheat cereal, crushed
1 tablespoon grated Parmesan cheese
¾ teaspoon garlic salt

Cook noodles as directed on package; drain. Cut bologna into ⅜-inch slices. Cook and stir bologna, onion, celery and green pepper in oil in 10-inch skillet over medium heat until onion is tender. Stir in tomato sauce and chili powder.

Layer half each of the bologna mixture, noodles, beans (with liquid), olives and corn (with liquid) in greased 3-quart casserole; repeat. Spoon soup over top. Mix cereal, Parmesan cheese and garlic salt; sprinkle over soup. Cook uncovered in 350° oven until hot and bubbly, about 40 minutes.

9 servings.

LAMB CASSEROLE

2 small onions, thinly sliced
¼ cup vegetable oil
1 pound lamb for stew, cut into ½-inch pieces
1 small eggplant (about 1 pound), cut crosswise into slices
Salt and pepper
1 can (8 ounces) cut green beans, drained
2 medium carrots, sliced
1 large green pepper, cut into rings
4 medium tomatoes, cut into ½-inch slices
2 cups cooked rice
1 cup shredded Cheddar cheese (about 4 ounces)
Paprika
2 tablespoons snipped parsley

Cook and stir onions in oil in 10-inch skillet until onions are tender; remove from skillet. Cook and stir lamb in same skillet until brown; drain.

Arrange eggplant slices in ungreased 13x9x2-inch baking dish; top with lamb. Sprinkle with salt and pepper. Layer onions, beans, carrots, green pepper and tomatoes on lamb. Sprinkle with salt and pepper. Cover and cook until lamb is tender, about 1 hour.

Arrange rice by ½ cupfuls in 4 diagonal strips on casserole. Top rice with cheese; sprinkle with paprika. Cook uncovered until cheese is melted, 15 to 20 minutes. Sprinkle with parsley.

6 to 8 servings.

MOUSSAKA

1 medium eggplant (1½ to 2 pounds), cut crosswise into ½-inch slices
1 pound ground lamb or beef
2 tablespoons instant minced onion
2 tablespoons margarine or butter
3 cans (8 ounces each) tomato sauce
½ cup red Burgundy or other dry red wine or beef broth
1 tablespoon parsley flakes
1½ teaspoons salt
¼ teaspoon pepper
¼ teaspoon ground nutmeg
White Sauce (right)
1 egg, beaten
¾ cup grated Parmesan cheese
½ cup dry bread crumbs

Heat small amount salted water (½ teaspoon salt to 1 cup water) to boiling. Add eggplant. Cover and heat to boiling. Cook until tender, 5 to 8 minutes; drain.

Cook and stir lamb and onion in margarine in 10-inch skillet until lamb is brown. Stir in 1 can tomato sauce, the Burgundy, parsley, salt, pepper and nutmeg. Cook uncovered over medium heat until half of the liquid is absorbed, about 20 minutes. Prepare White Sauce.

Stir egg, ½ cup of the cheese and ¼ cup of the bread crumbs into lamb mixture; remove from heat. Sprinkle remaining bread crumbs evenly in ungreased 2½-quart casserole or 8x8x2-inch baking dish. Arrange half of the eggplant slices in casserole; top with lamb mixture. Sprinkle 2 tablespoons of the remaining cheese over lamb; top with remaining eggplant slices. Pour White Sauce over top; sprinkle with remaining cheese. Cook uncovered in 375° oven until hot and bubbly, about 45 minutes. Let stand 20 minutes before serving. Heat remaining tomato sauce until hot. Cut Moussaka into squares; serve with tomato sauce.

6 servings.

WHITE SAUCE

3 tablespoons margarine or butter
3 tablespoons all-purpose flour
½ teaspoon salt
¼ teaspoon ground nutmeg
2 eggs
1¾ cups milk
¼ cup grated Parmesan cheese

Heat margarine in saucepan until melted. Stir in flour, salt and nutmeg. Cook over low heat, stirring constantly, until smooth and bubbly; remove from heat. Mix eggs and milk; stir into flour mixture. Heat to boiling, stirring constantly. Boil and stir 1 minute. Stir in cheese; heat through.

Do-ahead Note: Before cooking, cover and refrigerate no longer than 24 hours. To serve, cook uncovered in 375° oven 45 minutes. Let stand 20 minutes before cutting.

CURRIED LAMB AND BARLEY CASSEROLE

1 pound lamb boneless shoulder, cut into 1-inch cubes
1 can (16 ounces) whole tomatoes
2 cups water
¾ cup uncooked barley
1 tablespoon plus 1 teaspoon instant minced onion
1 tablespoon parsley flakes
2 teaspoons salt
½ teaspoon curry powder

Mix lamb, tomatoes (with liquid) and the remaining ingredients in ungreased 2½-quart casserole or 9x9x2-inch pan. Cover and cook in 350° oven until barley is tender and liquid is absorbed, about 2 hours.

6 servings.

LAMB STEW

1½ pounds lamb boneless shoulder,
      cut into 2-inch cubes
1   tablespoon shortening
2   medium onions, chopped (about
      1 cup)
2   cups beef bouillon
3   medium potatoes, thinly sliced
1   teaspoon salt
¼   teaspoon pepper
¼   teaspoon celery seed
¼   teaspoon dried marjoram leaves
⅛   teaspoon dried thyme leaves
1   package (10 ounces) frozen green
      peas, rinsed and drained

Cook and stir lamb in shortening in 10-inch skillet until brown; drain. Add onions; cook and stir until tender. Stir in bouillon.

OVEN METHOD: Pour into ungreased 3-quart casserole or 13x9x2-inch baking dish. Cover and cook in 325° oven until lamb is tender, 2 to 2½ hours. Skim off excess fat. Stir in remaining ingredients. Cover and cook until vegetables are tender, 30 to 40 minutes.

RANGE-TOP METHOD: Heat to boiling; reduce heat. Cover and simmer 2 hours. Stir in potatoes and seasonings. Cover and simmer 30 minutes. Skim off excess fat. Stir in peas. Cover and simmer 10 minutes longer.

6 servings.

ORIENTAL-STYLE VEAL CASSEROLE

2   tablespoons shortening
1   pound veal boneless shoulder,
      cut into 1-inch cubes
2   tablespoons all-purpose flour
2   large stalks celery, sliced (about
      1½ cups)
1   medium onion, chopped (about
      ½ cup)
1   can (10¾ ounces) condensed
      cream of chicken soup
1   can (10¾ ounces) condensed
      cream of mushroom soup
1¼ cups water
2   to 3 tablespoons soy sauce
½   cup uncooked regular rice

Heat shortening in 10-inch skillet until hot. Coat veal with flour. Cook and stir veal in hot shortening until brown. Stir in remaining ingredients.

OVEN METHOD: Pour into ungreased 3-quart casserole or 13x9x2-inch baking dish. Cover and cook in 325° oven until rice is tender and liquid is absorbed, about 1½ hours. Sprinkle with cashews and serve with soy sauce if desired.

RANGE-TOP METHOD: Heat to boiling; reduce heat. Cover and simmer, stirring occasionally, until rice is tender and liquid is absorbed, about 30 minutes. Sprinkle with cashews and serve with soy sauce if desired.

5 or 6 servings.

Oriental-style Lamb Casserole: Substitute 1 pound lamb boneless shoulder, cut into 1-inch cubes, for the veal.

Do-ahead Note: Prepare as directed for Oven Method except—decrease cooking time to 1 hour. Cover and refrigerate no longer than 24 hours. To serve, cook uncovered in 325° oven 50 minutes.

Poultry Casseroles

CHICKEN-BROCCOLI CASSEROLE

2 tablespoons vegetable oil
2 tablespoons margarine or butter
6 small chicken breast halves (about 2 pounds)
½ teaspoon garlic salt
1 can (10¾ ounces) condensed cream of chicken soup
1 can (4 ounces) mushroom stems and pieces
¼ cup water
1 teaspoon Worcestershire sauce
½ teaspoon dried thyme leaves
2 packages (10 ounces each) frozen broccoli spears
½ teaspoon salt

Heat oil and margarine in 13x9x2-inch baking dish in 400° oven until margarine is melted. Place chicken in dish, turning to coat with margarine mixture. Arrange chicken skin sides up; sprinkle with garlic salt. Cook uncovered 30 minutes.

Mix soup, mushrooms (with liquid), water, Worcestershire sauce and thyme. Rinse broccoli under running cold water to separate; drain. Remove chicken from oven; drain fat from dish. Arrange broccoli around chicken; sprinkle with salt. Spoon soup mixture over broccoli. Cook uncovered until chicken is done and broccoli is tender, about 30 minutes. Garnish with paprika and ripe olives if desired.

6 servings.

■ **To Microwave:** Pierce frozen broccoli packages. Place side by side on paper plate and microwave on high (100%) 10 minutes. Arrange chicken breast halves, skin sides up, with thickest parts to outside in 12x7½x2-inch microwaveproof baking dish. Sprinkle with garlic salt. Cover loosely and microwave 10 minutes; drain. Arrange chicken in center and broccoli around chicken; sprinkle with salt. Mix soup mixture as directed; pour over chicken and broccoli. Cover loosely and microwave until chicken is done, 9 to 13 minutes longer.

CHICKEN BREASTS WITH RICE

4 small chicken breast halves (about
   1½ pounds)
½ teaspoon seasoned salt
1 jar (2½ ounces) sliced dried beef,
   cut up
2 medium stalks celery, chopped
   (about 1 cup)
1 small onion, chopped (about ¼
   cup)
¼ cup margarine or butter
2 cups cooked rice
2 tablespoons snipped parsley
1 jar (1 ounce) pine nuts (optional)

Place chicken, skin sides up, in ungreased 10x6x1½-inch pan. Sprinkle with seasoned salt. Roast uncovered in 400° oven 30 minutes.

Cook and stir beef, celery, onion and margarine in 8-inch skillet until celery is tender; remove from heat. Stir in rice, parsley and nuts. Remove chicken and drain fat from pan. Spoon rice mixture into pan; place chicken on top. Roast uncovered until chicken is golden brown and done, about 15 minutes.

4 servings.

■ **To Microwave:** Decrease margarine to 1 tablespoon. Place beef, celery, onion and margarine in 2-quart microwaveproof casserole. Cover tightly and microwave on high (100%) until onion is crisp-tender, 3 to 4 minutes. Stir in rice, parsley and nuts. Arrange chicken, skin sides up, on rice with thickest parts to outside edge of casserole. Sprinkle with seasoned salt and paprika. Cover tightly and microwave 5 minutes; rotate casserole ½ turn. Microwave until chicken is done, 8 to 11 minutes longer.

ORANGE CHICKEN WITH BROWN RICE

2½- to 3½-pound broiler-fryer
    chicken
2 tablespoons vegetable oil
2 tablespoons margarine or butter
¼ cup all-purpose flour
½ teaspoon salt
½ teaspoon paprika
⅛ teaspoon pepper
4 cups cooked brown rice
1 medium onion, thinly sliced
1 small green pepper, chopped
1 jar (4 ounces) sliced
   mushrooms, drained
1 cup orange juice
¼ cup dry white wine or apple juice
1 tablespoon packed brown sugar
1 teaspoon salt

Cut chicken into pieces; cut each breast half into halves. Heat oil and margarine in 13x9x2-inch baking dish in 425° oven until margarine is melted. Mix flour, ½ teaspoon salt, the paprika and pepper; coat chicken. Place chicken, skin sides down, in baking dish. Cook uncovered 30 minutes.

Remove chicken from dish; pour off fat. Place rice in baking dish; arrange onion, green pepper and mushrooms on top. Arrange chicken, skin sides up, on vegetables. Mix remaining ingredients; pour over top. Cover and cook until chicken is done, about 30 minutes longer. Garnish with orange slices if desired.

6 servings.

Pictured at right: Orange Chicken with Brown Rice (above)—an imaginative yet simple combo, ideal for family or company.

CHICKEN AND CURRY SAUCE

2½- to 3½-pound broiler-fryer
    chicken
  1 can (20 ounces) sliced pineapple
 ¼ cup soy sauce
  2 teaspoons ground ginger
 ¼ teaspoon pepper
 ¼ cup shortening
 ½ cup all-purpose flour
  3 cups cooked rice
 ¾ cup raisins
 ¼ cup toasted chopped almonds
    Curry Sauce (below)

Cut chicken into pieces; cut each breast half into halves. Drain pineapple, reserving ⅓ cup syrup. Mix reserved pineapple syrup, the soy sauce, ginger and pepper. Place chicken in large glass dish; pour syrup mixture over top. Cover and refrigerate, turning chicken occasionally, no longer than 12 hours.

Heat shortening in 10-inch skillet until hot. Remove chicken from dish, reserving 3 table-spoons of the marinade. Coat chicken with flour. Cook chicken in hot shortening until brown, 15 to 20 minutes.

Mix rice, raisins and almonds in ungreased 11x7x1½-inch baking dish. Top with pineapple slices and chicken; sprinkle with reserved marinade. Cover and cook in 350° oven 40 minutes. Uncover and cook until chicken is done, about 10 minutes longer. Serve with Curry Sauce.

6 servings.

CURRY SAUCE

  1 tablespoon margarine or butter
  1 tablespoon all-purpose flour
  1 tablespoon instant minced onion
 ½ teaspoon curry powder
 ¼ teaspoon ground ginger
 ⅛ teaspoon garlic powder
  1 cup milk
 ¼ cup toasted coconut

Heat margarine over low heat until melted. Stir in flour, onion, curry powder, ginger and garlic powder. Cook, stirring constantly, until bubbly; remove from heat. Stir in milk. Heat to boiling, stirring constantly. Boil and stir 1 minute. Stir in coconut; heat through.

MEXICAN-STYLE CHICKEN

2½- to 3½-pound broiler-fryer
    chicken
  3 tablespoons vegetable oil
 ½ cup all-purpose flour
  1 can (28 ounces) whole tomatoes
  1 medium onion, chopped (about
    ½ cup)
1½ teaspoons salt
1½ to 2 teaspoons chili powder
 ⅛ teaspoon instant minced garlic
 ⅛ teaspoon pepper
    Dash of cayenne pepper
  2 chicken bouillon cubes or 2
    teaspoons instant chicken
    bouillon
2½ cups boiling water
  1 cup uncooked regular rice
  1 can (8 ounces) whole kernel corn
  1 can (8 ounces) kidney beans

Cut chicken into pieces; cut each breast half into halves. Heat oil in 4-quart Dutch oven or 10-inch skillet. Coat chicken with flour. Cook in hot oil over medium heat until brown, 15 to 20 minutes; drain.

Mix tomatoes (with liquid) and the remaining ingredients except rice, corn and beans; pour over chicken.

OVEN METHOD: Cover and cook in 350° oven 30 minutes. Stir in rice, corn (with liquid) and beans (with liquid). Cover and cook until chicken is done and vegetables are hot, 30 to 40 minutes.

RANGE-TOP METHOD: Heat to boiling; reduce heat. Cover and simmer 20 minutes. Stir in rice, corn (with liquid) and beans (with liquid). Cover and simmer until chicken is done and vegetables are hot, 30 to 40 minutes.

6 servings.

CHICKEN AND DRESSING

2½- to 3½-pound broiler-fryer
     chicken
  ¼ cup vegetable oil
  ½ cup all-purpose flour
  1 teaspoon salt
  ½ teaspoon paprika
  ¼ teaspoon pepper
  1 can (10¾ ounces) condensed
     cream of chicken or cream of
     mushroom soup
  6 cups soft bread cubes
  1 cup milk
  1 medium onion, chopped (about
     ½ cup)
  ¾ cup chopped celery
  ¼ cup margarine or butter, melted
  1 teaspoon salt
  ½ teaspoon sage
  ½ teaspoon dried thyme leaves
  ¼ teaspoon pepper

Cut chicken into pieces; cut each breast half into halves. Heat oil in 10-inch skillet until hot. Mix flour, 1 teaspoon salt, the paprika and ¼ teaspoon pepper; coat chicken. Cook chicken in hot oil over medium heat until brown, 15 to 20 minutes. Place in ungreased 2½-quart casserole or 13x9x2-inch baking dish. Pour soup over chicken.

Toss remaining ingredients. Mound mixture on chicken. Cover and cook in 350° oven until chicken is done; 1 to 1¼ hours.

6 servings.

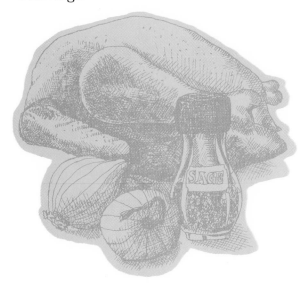

OVEN CHICKEN WITH MACARONI

2½- to 3½-pound broiler-fryer
     chicken
  ¼ cup shortening
  ½ cup all-purpose flour
  1 teaspoon salt
  1 teaspoon parsley flakes
  ¼ teaspoon pepper
  1 can (4 ounces) mushroom stems
     and pieces
  1 can (10¾ ounces) condensed
     cream of celery soup
  1 cup milk
  1 teaspoon dried oregano leaves
  1 package (7 ounces) elbow
     macaroni
  1 package (10 ounces) frozen green
     peas
  2 tablespoons chopped pimiento
    Paprika

Cut chicken into pieces; cut each breast half into halves. Heat shortening in 10-inch skillet over medium heat until melted. Mix flour, salt, parsley and pepper; coat chicken. Cook chicken in hot shortening until brown, 15 to 20 minutes. Remove chicken; reserve. Stir in mushrooms (with liquid), soup, milk and oregano until smooth. Remove from heat.

Cook macaroni as directed on package; drain. Rinse peas under running cold water to separate; drain. Place macaroni in ungreased 3-quart casserole or 13x9x2-inch baking dish. Mix in peas, pimiento and half of the soup mixture. Arrange chicken pieces on macaroni mixture; pour remaining soup mixture over chicken. Sprinkle with paprika. Cover and cook in 375° oven 50 minutes. Uncover and cook until thickest pieces are done, about 10 minutes longer.

6 servings.

FESTIVE CHICKEN

2½- to 3½-pound broiler-fryer
      chicken
½ cup all-purpose flour
1 teaspoon salt
¼ teaspoon pepper
¼ cup vegetable oil
1 large onion, chopped (about
      ¾ cup)
1 green pepper, chopped
¼ cup raisins or currants
1 clove garlic, finely chopped, or ⅛
      teaspoon garlic powder
1 can (16 ounces) whole tomatoes,
      broken up
1½ teaspoons curry powder
½ teaspoon dried thyme leaves
¼ teaspoon salt
⅓ cup toasted slivered blanched
      almonds

Cut chicken into pieces; cut each breast half into halves. Mix flour, 1 teaspoon salt and the pepper; coat chicken. Heat oil in 10-inch skillet until hot. Cook chicken in hot oil over medium heat until brown, 15 to 20 minutes. Place in ungreased 13x9x2-inch baking dish or 2½-quart casserole.

Drain oil from skillet. Add onion, green pepper, raisins, garlic, tomatoes (with liquid), curry powder, thyme and ¼ teaspoon salt to skillet. Heat to boiling, stirring frequently to loosen brown particles from skillet. Pour over chicken. Cover and cook in 350° oven until thickest pieces are done, about 40 minutes. Skim fat from liquid if necessary. Cook uncovered 5 minutes longer. Sprinkle with almonds. Serve with chutney if desired.

6 servings.

Festive Chicken—a new treatment for the flavors of India.

CHICKEN CACCIATORE CASSEROLE

2½- to 3½-pound broiler-fryer
  chicken
 2 tablespoons vegetable oil
 2 tablespoons margarine or butter
 ½ cup all-purpose flour
 1 teaspoon salt
 ½ teaspoon paprika
 ¼ teaspoon pepper
 1 package (7 ounces) spaghetti
 1 can (16 ounces) whole tomatoes
 1 can (8 ounces) tomato sauce
 1 cup sliced mushrooms
 ¼ cup sliced pitted ripe olives
 1 medium onion, chopped (about
  ½ cup)
 1 clove garlic, finely chopped
 ¼ cup water
 1 teaspoon salt
 1 teaspoon dried oregano leaves
 ¼ teaspoon pepper

Cut chicken into pieces; cut each breast half into halves. Heat oil and margarine in 13x9x2-inch baking dish in 425° oven until margarine is melted. Mix flour, 1 teaspoon salt, the paprika and ¼ teaspoon pepper; coat chicken. Place chicken, skin sides down, in baking dish. Cook uncovered 30 minutes

Cook spaghetti as directed on package; drain. Remove chicken from dish; pour off fat. Place spaghetti in baking dish. Arrange chicken, skin sides up, on spaghetti. Mix tomatoes (with liquid) and the remaining ingredients; break up tomatoes with fork. Pour over chicken and spaghetti. Cover and cook until chicken is done, about 30 minutes. Garnish with parsley if desired.

6 servings.

CHICKEN-SPINACH CASSEROLE

 3 cups soft bread cubes
 1 cup cut-up cooked chicken or
  turkey
 1 package (10 ounces) frozen
  chopped spinach, thawed and
  very well drained
 ¾ cup dairy sour cream
 1 can (4 ounces) mushroom stems
  and pieces, drained
 2 tablespoons finely chopped onion
 1 medium clove garlic, finely
  chopped
 ¾ teaspoon salt
 ¼ teaspoon dry mustard
 3 eggs, separated
 3 tablespoons margarine or butter,
  melted
 ½ teaspoon poppy seed

Heat oven to 350°. Mix 1½ cups of the bread cubes, the chicken, spinach, sour cream, mushrooms, onion, garlic, salt, mustard and egg yolks. Beat egg whites until stiff but not dry; fold into chicken mixture. Pour into greased 1½-quart casserole. Toss remaining bread cubes, the margarine and poppy seed; sprinkle over chicken mixture. Cook uncovered until center is set and top is golden, about 45 minutes.

5 servings.

Adding Chicken Broth?

Some cooks always have a container or two of chicken broth in the freezer. Most don't. If you're among the latter, you can rely on canned broth or its instant form to fill the bill:

■ 1 can (10¾ ounces) condensed chicken broth plus 1 soup can water yields about 2½ cups chicken broth.

■ 1 teaspoon instant chicken bouillon or 1 cube chicken bouillon plus 1 cup water yields 1 cup chicken broth.

CHICKEN DINNER CASSEROLE

1 package (10 ounces) frozen peas
    and carrots
1 can (8 ounces) small whole onions,
    drained
1 can (4 ounces) mushroom stems
    and pieces
1 can (10¾ ounces) condensed
    cream of chicken soup
2 cups cut-up cooked chicken or
    turkey
1 cup crushed potato chips

Rinse frozen peas and carrots under running cold water to separate; drain.

OVEN METHOD: Mix peas and carrots, onions, mushrooms (with liquid), soup and chicken in ungreased 2-quart casserole or 8x8x2-inch baking dish. Sprinkle with chips. Cook uncovered in 350° oven until hot and bubbly, 35 to 40 minutes.

RANGE-TOP METHOD: Mix peas and carrots, onions, mushrooms (with liquid), soup and chicken in 2-quart saucepan. Heat to boiling; reduce heat. Cover and simmer, stirring occasionally, until vegetables are done, 8 to 10 minutes. Sprinkle with chips.

6 servings.

■ **To Microwave:** Mix peas and carrots, onions, mushrooms (with liquid), soup and chicken in 2-quart microwaveproof casserole. Cover tightly and microwave on high (100%) 5 minutes; stir. Cover and microwave until hot, 5 to 7 minutes longer. Sprinkle with chips.

CHICKEN ALMOND CASSEROLE

4 cups cut-up cooked chicken or
    turkey
1 can (4 ounces) mushroom stems
    and pieces, drained
1 can (8 ounces) water chestnuts,
    drained and cut crosswise into
    halves
⅔ cup blanched whole almonds
1 medium onion, chopped (about ½
    cup)
    Chicken Sauce (below)
    Paprika

Spread 2 cups of the chicken in ungreased 2-quart casserole or 12x7½x2-inch baking dish. Top with mushrooms, water chestnuts, almonds and onion. Spread with remaining chicken. Pour Chicken Sauce over top; sprinkle with paprika. Cook uncovered in 350° oven until hot and bubbly, about 45 minutes. Serve with cranberry-orange relish if desired.

6 to 8 servings.

CHICKEN SAUCE

¼ cup margarine or butter
¼ cup all-purpose flour
½ teaspoon salt
¼ teaspoon pepper
1 cup chicken broth
¾ cup milk
2 tablespoons dry white wine

Heat margarine in saucepan over low heat until melted. Stir in flour, salt and pepper. Cook, stirring constantly, until smooth and bubbly; remove from heat. Stir in broth and milk. Heat to boiling, stirring constantly. Boil and stir 1 minute; remove from heat. Stir in wine.

CHICKEN-MACARONI CASSEROLE

1 package (7 ounces) elbow
   macaroni
1 cup shredded Cheddar cheese
   (about 4 ounces)
1½ cups cut-up cooked chicken or
   turkey
1 can (4 ounces) mushroom stems
   and pieces (with liquid)
1 jar (2 ounces) diced pimiento
1 can (10¾ ounces) condensed
   cream of chicken soup
1 cup milk
½ teaspoon salt
½ teaspoon curry powder

OVEN METHOD: Mix all ingredients in ungreased 1½-quart casserole or 10x6x1½-inch baking dish. Cover and cook in 350° oven until macaroni is tender, 55 to 60 minutes.

RANGE-TOP METHOD: Mix all ingredients in 10-inch skillet. Heat to boiling, stirring occasionally; reduce heat. Cover and simmer, stirring occasionally, until macaroni is tender, about 15 minutes.

4 to 6 servings.

■ **To Microwave:** Mix all ingredients in 3-quart microwaveproof casserole. Cover tightly and microwave on high (100%), stirring every 6 minutes, until macaroni is tender, 15 to 18 minutes. Let stand 5 minutes.

CHICKEN TETRAZZINI

7 ounces spaghetti, broken into
   small pieces
¼ cup margarine or butter
¼ cup all-purpose flour
½ teaspoon salt
¼ teaspoon pepper
1 cup chicken broth
1 cup whipping cream or half-and-
   half
2 tablespoons sherry
2 cups cut-up cooked chicken or
   turkey
1 can (4 ounces) mushroom stems
   and pieces, drained
½ cup grated Parmesan cheese

Cook spaghetti as directed on package; drain. Heat margarine in 3-quart saucepan until melted. Stir in flour, salt and pepper. Cook, stirring constantly, until smooth and bubbly; remove from heat. Stir in broth and cream. Heat to boiling, stirring constantly. Boil and stir 1 minute. Stir in spaghetti, sherry, chicken and mushrooms. Pour into ungreased 2-quart casserole or 8x8x2-inch baking dish. Sprinkle with cheese. Cook uncovered in 350° oven until top is golden brown, about 30 minutes.

6 servings.

Do-ahead Note: Before cooking, cover and refrigerate no longer than 24 hours. To serve, cook uncovered in 350° oven 45 to 50 minutes.

CHEESE PUFF ON CREAMED CHICKEN

1 package (10 ounces) frozen green
   peas
2 cups cut-up cooked chicken or
   turkey
1 can (10¾ ounces) condensed
   cream of chicken soup
1 cup dairy sour cream
½ teaspoon salt
⅛ teaspoon pepper
1 tablespoon snipped parsley
1 tablespoon chopped pimiento
1 cup all-purpose flour
2 teaspoons baking powder
1 teaspoon salt
2 eggs, beaten
½ cup milk
1 cup shredded Cheddar cheese
   (about 4 ounces)
1 tablespoon snipped parsley
1 tablespoon chopped pimiento
¼ cup shredded Cheddar cheese
¼ cup milk

Heat oven to 350°. Rinse frozen peas under running cold water to separate; drain. Place peas and chicken in 2-quart casserole or 12x7½x2-inch baking dish. Heat soup, sour cream, salt and pepper just to boiling, stirring constantly. Stir in 1 tablespoon parsley and 1 tablespoon pimiento. Stir 1½ cups of the soup mixture into peas and chicken. Place in oven while preparing topping.

Mix flour, baking powder and salt. Stir in eggs, ½ cup milk, 1 cup cheese, 1 tablespoon parsley and 1 tablespoon pimiento just until blended. Drop by spoonfuls onto hot chicken mixture. Sprinkle with ¼ cup cheese. Cook uncovered until topping is puffed and golden, casserole 40 to 45 minutes, baking dish 25 to 30 minutes. Heat ¼ cup milk and the remaining soup mixture; serve with cheese puff.

6 to 8 servings.

CHICKEN WITH PHYLLO

¼ cup margarine or butter
¼ cup all-purpose flour
1 tablespoon dry mustard
1 teaspoon salt
¼ teaspoon pepper
2 cups milk
1 package (8 ounces) cream cheese,
   cut into ½-inch pieces
1 package (10 ounces) frozen green
   peas
2 cups cut-up cooked chicken or
   turkey
2 medium stalks celery, sliced
   (about 1 cup)
½ cup sliced green onions (with
   tops)
6 frozen phyllo sheets, thawed
¼ cup margarine or butter, melted

Heat ¼ cup margarine in 3-quart saucepan over low heat until melted. Blend in flour, mustard, salt and pepper. Cook over low heat, stirring constantly, until smooth and bubbly; remove from heat. Stir in milk. Heat to boiling, stirring constantly. Boil and stir 1 minute. Remove from heat; stir in cream cheese. Beat until smooth.

Rinse frozen peas under running cold water to separate; drain. Stir peas, chicken, celery and onions into sauce. Spread in ungreased 8x8x2-inch baking dish.

Cut phyllo sheets crosswise into halves; cover with damp towel to keep them from drying out. Carefully separate 1 half-sheet; place on chicken mixture, folding edges under to fit dish if necessary. Brush with melted margarine. Repeat with remaining 11 half-sheets. Brush top with melted margarine. Cut top into 6 servings. Cook uncovered in 375° oven until golden brown, about 45 minutes. Let stand 10 minutes before serving.

6 servings.

Cut sheets crosswise into halves.   Handle gently to avoid tearing.   Cut through top before baking.

Chicken with Phyllo (left)—a delicate, creamy filling with a flaky pastry topping.

CREAMED CHICKEN AND CORN BREAD

¼ cup margarine or butter
¼ cup all-purpose flour
½ teaspoon salt
⅛ teaspoon pepper
1 cup water
1 cup milk
1 teaspoon instant chicken bouillon
2 cups cut-up cooked chicken or turkey
1 small green pepper, chopped (about ½ cup)
1 can (4 ounces) mushroom stems and pieces
1 jar (2 ounces) diced pimiento
Corn Bread (below)

Heat margarine in 2-quart saucepan over low heat until melted. Stir in flour, salt and pepper. Cook, stirring constantly, until smooth and bubbly; remove from heat. Stir in water, milk and instant bouillon. Heat to boiling, stirring constantly. Boil and stir 1 minute. Stir in chicken, green pepper, mushrooms (with liquid) and pimiento (with liquid).

Prepare Corn Bread. Pour hot chicken mixture into ungreased 8x8x2-inch baking dish. Pour Corn Bread batter over top. Cook uncovered in 450° oven until golden brown, 25 to 30 minutes.

6 servings.

CORN BREAD

¾ cup cornmeal
¼ cup all-purpose flour
1½ teaspoons baking powder
½ teaspoon sugar
½ teaspoon salt
¼ teaspoon baking soda
2 tablespoons vegetable oil
¾ cup buttermilk
1 egg

Mix all ingredients; beat vigorously 30 seconds.

CHICKEN AND BISCUITS

1 package (10 ounces) frozen green peas
2 cups cut-up cooked chicken or turkey
1 can (10¾ ounces) condensed cream of chicken soup
½ cup dairy sour cream
½ cup milk
½ teaspoon salt
⅛ teaspoon pepper
2 cups buttermilk baking mix
½ cup cold water
1¼ cups shredded process American or Cheddar cheese (about 5 ounces)

Heat oven to 425°. Rinse peas under running cold water to separate; drain. Heat peas, chicken, soup, sour cream, ½ cup milk, the salt and pepper just to boiling in 3-quart saucepan, stirring frequently. Reduce heat; keep warm while preparing biscuits.

Mix baking mix and water until soft dough forms; beat vigorously 20 strokes. Gently smooth dough into a ball on floured cloth-covered board. Knead 5 times. Roll dough ½ inch thick. Cut with floured 2-inch cutter. Pour chicken mixture into ungreased 2-quart casserole or 12x7½x2-inch baking dish. Sprinkle with cheese. Place biscuits on cheese. Cook uncovered until biscuits are golden brown, about 20 minutes.

6 servings.

Yields for Cooked Poultry

When it comes to cooking chicken or turkey, it's a good idea to cook more than you need for a single meal. Leftovers are great for casseroles. Here's what you'll get:

Kind and Size	Approximate Cooked Amount
3- to 4-pound broiler-fryer chicken	3 to 4 cups
5- to 6-pound turkey breast	10 to 12 cups
12-pound turkey	About 14 cups

CHICKEN AND HOMINY CASEROLE

1 can (20 ounces) hominy, drained
2 cups cut-up cooked chicken or turkey
½ cup sliced pitted ripe olives
1 can (10¾ ounces) condensed cream of chicken soup
1 can (4 ounces) chopped green chilies
1 jar (2 ounces) diced pimiento
½ cup dairy sour cream
½ teaspoon salt
½ teaspoon ground cumin
2 cups tortilla chips or potato chips, coarsely crushed (about 1 cup)

Place hominy in ungreased 2-quart casserole or 8x8x2-inch baking dish. Top with chicken and olives. Mix soup, chilies (with liquid), pimiento (with liquid), the sour cream, salt and cumin; spread over chicken. Sprinkle with chips. Cook uncovered in 350° oven until hot, about 45 minutes.

6 servings.

Chicken and Corn Casserole: Substitute 1 can (17 ounces) whole kernel corn, drained, for the hominy.

■ **To Microwave:** Prepare as directed in 2-quart microwaveproof casserole except—do not sprinkle with chips. Cover tightly and microwave on high (100%) 8 minutes; rotate casserole ½ turn. Cover and microwave until center is hot, 6 to 8 minutes longer. Sprinkle with chips.

CHICKEN PUFF

1 can (10¾ ounces) condensed cream of mushroom soup
⅓ cup milk
1 cup cut-up cooked chicken or turkey
1 can (16 ounces) cut green beans, drained
4 eggs, separated
¼ cup shredded process American cheese

Heat oven to 375°. Mix soup, milk, chicken and beans in ungreased 1½-quart casserole. Cook uncovered 10 minutes. Beat egg yolks until thick and lemon colored, about 5 minutes. Stir in cheese. Beat egg whites until stiff; fold in cheese mixture. Spoon onto hot chicken mixture. Cook uncovered until topping is puffy and golden, about 35 minutes.

6 servings.

CHICKEN 'N STUFFING BAKE

3 cups cut-up cooked chicken or turkey
3½ cups herb-seasoned croutons
1 medium stalk celery, chopped
1 medium onion, chopped (about ½ cup)
½ cup water
⅓ cup margarine or butter, melted
1 can (10¾ ounces) condensed cream of chicken soup
¼ cup water

Place chicken in ungreased 2-quart casserole or 9x9x2-inch pan. Toss croutons, celery and onion with ½ cup water and the margarine until croutons are moistened. Reserve about 1½ cups of the stuffing; spread remaining stuffing over chicken. Mix soup and ¼ cup water; pour over stuffing. Top with reserved stuffing. Cook uncovered in 350° oven until hot, about 30 minutes.

6 servings.

■ **To Microwave:** Prepare as directed in 2-quart microwaveproof casserole. Cover tightly and microwave on high (100%) 5 minutes; rotate casserole ½ turn. Cover and microwave until hot in center, 7 to 10 minutes longer.

HOT CHICKEN SALAD

2 cups cut-up cooked chicken or
      turkey
2 cups seasoned croutons
2 cups thinly sliced celery
1 cup mayonnaise or salad dressing
½ cup toasted slivered almonds
1 small onion, chopped (about ¼ cup)
2 tablespoons lemon juice
½ teaspoon salt
½ cup shredded process American or
      Cheddar cheese

Mix all ingredients except cheese in un-greased 2-quart casserole or 12x7½x2-inch baking dish. Sprinkle with cheese. Cook uncovered in 350° oven until hot, 30 to 35 minutes.

6 servings.

Hot Tuna Salad: Substitute 2 cans (6½ ounces each) tuna, drained, for the chicken.

■ **To Microwave:** Mix all ingredients except cheese in 2-quart microwaveproof casserole. Sprinkle with cheese. Cover tightly and microwave on high (100%) 3 minutes; rotate casserole ½ turn. Microwave until hot, 4 to 6 minutes longer.

CHICKEN-GREEN BEAN CASSEROLE

1 can (16 ounces) Italian or
      French-style green beans
1 can (10¾ ounces) condensed
      cream of onion soup
2 cans (5 ounces each) boned
      chicken or 1½ cups cut-up
      cooked chicken or turkey
1 can (1¾ ounces) shoestring
      potatoes

OVEN METHOD: Drain beans, reserving ½ cup liquid. Mix beans, reserved liquid, soup and chicken in ungreased 2-quart casserole or 8x8x2-inch baking dish. Sprinkle with potatoes. Cook uncovered in 350° oven until hot and bubbly, 25 to 30 minutes.

RANGE-TOP METHOD: Drain beans, reserving ½ cup liquid. Mix beans, reserved liquid, soup and chicken in 2-quart saucepan. Heat over medium heat, stirring occasionally, until hot, about 5 minutes. Sprinkle with potatoes.

4 servings.

■ **To Microwave:** Omit reserved bean liquid. Mix beans, soup and chicken in 2-quart microwaveproof casserole. Cover tightly and microwave on high (100%) 5 minutes; stir. Cover and microwave until hot, 2 to 5 minutes longer. Sprinkle with potatoes.

CHICKEN-ASPARAGUS BAKE

1 package (10 ounces) frozen cut
      asparagus
1 package (2½ ounces) thinly sliced
      smoked chicken or turkey, cut up
½ teaspoon dried marjoram leaves
¼ to ½ teaspoon ground sage
1 cup shredded process American
      cheese (about 4 ounces)
½ cup milk
2 eggs, beaten
1 cup all-purpose flour
2 teaspoons baking powder
1 teaspoon salt
      Quick Cheese Sauce (below)

Cook asparagus as directed on package; drain. Arrange asparagus in ungreased 8x8x2-inch baking dish. Arrange chicken on asparagus; sprinkle with marjoram and sage.

Mix cheese, milk and eggs. Stir in flour, baking powder and salt; spread over chicken. Cook uncovered in 350° oven until golden brown, 25 to 30 minutes. Serve with Quick Cheese Sauce.

6 servings.

QUICK CHEESE SAUCE

1 can (11 ounces) condensed
      Cheddar cheese soup
⅓ cup milk
¼ teaspoon dry mustard
¼ teaspoon Worcestershire sauce

Heat all ingredients just to boiling, stirring frequently.

CHICKEN LIVERS AND RICE

3 small onions, chopped (about
 ¾ cup)
1 medium stalk celery, chopped
 (about ½ cup)
1 can (4 ounces) mushroom stems
 and pieces, drained, or 4 ounces
 fresh mushrooms, sliced
2 tablespoons margarine or butter
2 cans (10¾ ounces each)
 condensed chicken broth
1 package (6 ounces) long-grain and
 wild rice mix
4 slices bacon
1 pound chicken livers
¼ cup all-purpose flour

Cook and stir onion, celery and mushrooms in margarine in 2-quart saucepan until onion is tender. Stir in chicken broth; heat to boiling. Place rice and seasoning mix in ungreased 2-quart casserole or 12x7½x2-inch baking dish. Stir chicken broth mixture into rice. Cover and cook in 350° oven 30 minutes.

Fry bacon until crisp; drain and crumble. Coat livers with flour; cook and stir in bacon fat until brown. Arrange livers on rice around edge of casserole. Cover and cook until rice is tender and liquid is absorbed, about 25 minutes. Sprinkle with bacon.

4 to 6 servings.

COOKING RICE

For perfect rice, follow these cooking instructions and refer to the chart below for the right amounts:

Regular Rice: Heat rice, water and salt to boiling, stirring once or twice; reduce heat. Cover and simmer 14 minutes. (Do not lift cover or stir.) Remove from heat. Fluff rice lightly with fork; cover immediately and let steam 5 to 10 minutes.

Precooked (Instant) Rice: Follow the package directions.

Brown Rice: Follow directions for Regular Rice (left) except—increase cooking time to 30 to 40 minutes.

Wild Rice: Wash rice by placing in wire strainer; run cold water through it, lifting rice with fingers to clean thoroughly. Heat rice, water and salt to boiling, stirring once or twice; reduce heat. Cover and simmer until tender, 40 to 50 minutes. After cooking 30 minutes, check to see that rice is not sticking to pan. Add ¼ cup water if necessary.

Approximate Yield Cooked	Rice	Water	Salt
1 cup: Regular white rice	⅓ cup	⅔ cup	¼ teaspoon
Precooked (instant) rice	½ cup	½ cup	¼ teaspoon
1½ cups: Regular white rice	½ cup	1 cup	½ teaspoon
Precooked (instant) rice	¾ cup	¾ cup	¼ teaspoon
2 cups: Regular white rice	⅔ cup	1⅓ cups	½ teaspoon
Precooked (instant) rice	1 cup	1 cup	½ teaspoon
3 cups: Regular white rice	1 cup	2 cups	1 teaspoon
Precooked (instant) rice	1½ cups	1½ cups	1 teaspoon
Wild rice	1 cup	2½ cups	1 teaspoon
4 cups: Regular white rice	1⅓ cups	2⅔ cups	1 teaspoon
Precooked (instant) rice	2 cups	2 cups	1 teaspoon
Brown rice	1 cup	2½ cups	1 teaspoon

WILD RICE AND TURKEY CASSEROLE

    2 cups cut-up cooked turkey or
        chicken
    1 package (6 ounces) seasoned
        long grain and wild rice
    1 can (10¾ ounces) condensed
        cream of mushroom soup
    ⅓ cup milk
    1 small onion, chopped (about ¼
        cup)
    ½ teaspoon salt
    2¼ cups boiling water

OVEN METHOD: Mix all ingredients in un-greased 2-quart casserole or 8x8x2-inch baking dish. Cover and cook in 350° oven until rice is tender, about 50 minutes. Uncover and cook until liquid is absorbed, 10 to 15 minutes longer.

RANGE-TOP METHOD: Mix all ingredients in 10-inch skillet. Heat to boiling; reduce heat. Cover and simmer until rice is tender and liquid is absorbed, 25 to 30 minutes.

6 servings.

TURKEY AND EGG CASSEROLE

    2 cups cut-up cooked turkey or
        chicken
    1 can (10¾ ounces) condensed
        cream of chicken soup
    1 cup cooked rice
    2 medium stalks celery, chopped
        (about 1 cup)
    ¾ cup mayonnaise or salad dressing
    1 tablespoon lemon juice
    1 teaspoon instant minced onion
    ½ teaspoon salt
    1 cup crushed corn flake cereal
    2 tablespoons margarine or butter,
        melted
    3 hard-cooked eggs, sliced

Mix all ingredients except cereal, margarine and eggs in ungreased 1½-quart casserole or 10x6x1½-inch baking dish. Mix cereal and margarine; sprinkle over top. Cook uncovered in 375° oven until topping is golden brown, 25 to 30 minutes. Arrange eggs on top.

6 servings.

■ **To Microwave:** Prepare as directed in 2-quart microwaveproof casserole. Microwave uncovered on high (100%) 5 minutes; rotate casserole ½ turn. Microwave until hot, 3 to 5 minutes longer. Arrange eggs on top.

TURKEY-RICE CASSEROLE

    ¼ cup margarine or butter
    ⅓ cup all-purpose flour
    1½ teaspoons salt
    ⅛ teaspoon pepper
    1 cup chicken broth
    1½ cups milk
    1½ cups cooked white or wild rice
    2 cups cut-up cooked turkey or
        chicken
    1 jar (4 ounces) sliced
        mushrooms, drained
    ⅓ cup chopped green pepper
    2 tablespoons chopped pimiento
    ¼ cup slivered almonds

Heat margarine in 3-quart saucepan until melted. Stir in flour, salt and pepper. Cook over low heat, stirring constantly, until smooth and bubbly; remove from heat. Stir in broth and milk. Heat to boiling, stirring constantly. Boil and stir 1 minute. Stir in remaining ingredients.

OVEN METHOD: Pour into ungreased 1½-quart casserole. Cook uncovered in 350° oven until hot and bubbly, 40 to 45 minutes.

RANGE-TOP METHOD: Reduce heat. Simmer uncovered until hot, about 5 minutes.

6 to 8 servings.

■ **To Microwave:** Microwave margarine in 2-quart microwaveproof casserole on high (100%) until melted, about 45 seconds. Stir in flour, salt and pepper. Decrease milk to ½ cup. Stir broth and milk into flour mixture. Microwave, stirring every minute, until thickened, 4 to 5 minutes. Stir in remaining ingredients. Cover and microwave until hot and bubbly, 5 to 8 minutes.

DEEP DISH TURKEY PIE

- 1 can (23 ounces) vacuum-pack sweet potatoes
- 2 cups cut-up cooked turkey or chicken
- 1 medium onion, chopped (about ½ cup)
- 1 package (10 ounces) frozen green peas, broken apart
- 1 package (1 ounce) chicken gravy mix
- 1 teaspoon salt
- ½ teaspoon grated lemon peel
  Sweet Potato Biscuits (right)

Heat oven to 400°. Mash enough of the sweet potatoes to measure ¼ cup; reserve for Sweet Potato Biscuits. Cut remaining sweet potatoes into ½-inch slices.

Alternate layers of turkey, onion, frozen peas and sweet potato slices in ungreased 2-quart casserole. Prepare gravy mix as directed on package except—stir in salt and lemon peel. Pour into casserole. Cook uncovered 15 minutes.

Prepare Sweet Potato Biscuits dough. Drop half of the dough (5 to 7 spoonfuls) onto hot turkey pie. Cook uncovered until biscuits are light brown, about 20 minutes.

6 servings.

SWEET POTATO BISCUITS

- 3 tablespoons shortening
- 1 cup all-purpose flour
- ¼ cup mashed sweet potatoes
- 2 teaspoons sugar
- 2 teaspoons baking powder
- ½ teaspoon salt
- ¼ to ½ cup milk

Cut shortening into flour, sweet potatoes, sugar, baking powder and salt. Stir in milk. Divide dough into halves. Use one half for pie. Drop remaining dough by spoonfuls onto greased cookie sheet. Cool until light brown, 12 to 15 minutes.

Deep Dish Turkey Pie, with enough dough for biscuits on the side.

CRANBERRY WHIRLS OVER TURKEY

2 cans (10¾ ounces each) condensed cream of celery soup
¾ cup milk
1½ cups cooked vegetables
3 cups cut-up cooked turkey or chicken
2 cups buttermilk baking mix
½ cup cold water
½ cup cranberry sauce

Heat oven to 450°. Heat soup and milk in 3-quart saucepan, stirring frequently, until hot. Stir in vegetables and turkey; heat through. Mix baking mix and water until soft dough forms; beat vigorously 20 strokes. Gently smooth dough into a ball on floured cloth-covered board. Knead 5 times. Roll into rectangle, 12x9 inches; spread with cranberry sauce. Roll up, beginning at 12-inch side; cut into 1-inch slices.

Pour soup mixture into ungreased 3-quart casserole or 13x9x2-inch baking dish. Place slices, cut sides down, on hot soup mixture. Cook uncovered until biscuits are golden brown, about 20 minutes.

6 to 8 servings.

CLASSIC TURKEY DIVAN

¼ cup margarine or butter
¼ cup all-purpose flour
⅛ teaspoon ground nutmeg
1½ cups chicken broth
½ cup grated Parmesan cheese
2 tablespoons dry white wine
½ cup chilled whipping cream
1½ pounds fresh broccoli, cooked and drained, or 2 packages (10 ounces each) frozen broccoli spears, cooked and drained
5 large slices cooked turkey or chicken breast (about ¾ pound)
½ cup grated Parmesan cheese

Heat margarine in 1-quart saucepan over low heat until melted. Stir in flour and nutmeg. Cook, stirring constantly, until smooth and bubbly; remove from heat. Stir in broth. Heat to boiling, stirring constantly. Boil and stir 1 minute; remove from heat. Stir in ½ cup Parmesan cheese and the wine. Beat whipping cream in chilled bowl until stiff. Fold cheese sauce into whipped cream.

Arrange hot broccoli in ungreased 12x7½x2-inch baking dish; top with turkey. Pour cheese sauce over turkey; sprinkle with ½ cup Parmesan cheese. Set oven control to broil and/or 550°. Broil with top 3 to 5 inches from heat until cheese is bubbly and light brown.

5 servings.

Do-ahead Note: Before cooking, cover and refrigerate no longer than 24 hours. To serve, cook uncovered in 350° oven until hot, about 45 minutes.

■ **To Microwave:** Heat margarine in 1-quart microwaveproof measure on high (100%) until melted, 1 to 2 minutes. Decrease chicken broth to 1 cup. Stir in flour, nutmeg and broth. Microwave uncovered, stirring every minute, until sauce is thickened, 4 to 5 minutes. Continue as directed. Prepare casserole in 12x7½x2-inch microwaveproof baking dish. Cover tightly and microwave until hot, 5 to 7 minutes.

CRUNCHY FISH-NOODLE CASSEROLE

1½ cups flaked cooked fish
1 can (11 ounces) mandarin orange segments, drained
1 can (10¾ ounces) condensed cream of mushroom soup
1½ cups thinly sliced celery
1 medium onion, chopped (about ½ cup)
1 tablespoon soy sauce
½ teaspoon salt
1 cup chow mein noodles
½ cup cashews or salted peanuts

Spread flaked fish in ungreased 10x6x1½- or 8x8x2-inch baking dish. Reserve ⅓ cup of the orange segments; sprinkle remaining orange segments on fish. Mix soup, celery, onion, soy sauce and salt. Spread over fish and orange segments. Sprinkle with chow mein noodles and cashews. Cook uncovered in 350° oven until hot and bubbly, 30 to 35 minutes. Garnish with remaining orange segments.

6 servings.

■ **To Microwave:** Prepare as directed in 8x8x2-inch microwaveproof baking dish. Microwave uncovered on high (100%) until hot, 7 to 9 minutes.

FISH CASSEROLE, GREEK STYLE

12 ounces fish fillets, cut into 1-inch pieces
3 cups cooked rice
1 can (16 ounces) cut green beans, drained
1 medium onion, chopped (about ½ cup)
2 medium tomatoes, chopped (about 1½ cups)
1 teaspoon salt
½ teaspoon dried basil leaves
½ teaspoon dried oregano leaves
⅓ cup sliced pitted ripe olives
⅓ cup grated Parmesan cheese

Mix all ingredients except cheese in ungreased 1½-quart casserole or 10x6x1½-inch baking dish. Cover and cook in 350° oven 30 minutes. Sprinkle with cheese. Cook uncovered until fish flakes easily with fork, 5 to 10 minutes.

6 servings.

HAWAIIAN HALIBUT

1 pound halibut or haddock steaks
   or fillets
1 teaspoon salt
2 cups cooked rice
2 tablespoons lemon juice
1 teaspoon curry powder
2 cups soft bread cubes
1 can (20 ounces) crushed
   pineapple, drained

Cut fish into 4 to 6 serving pieces if necessary; place in ungreased 10x6x1½-inch baking dish. Sprinkle with salt. Mix rice, lemon juice and curry powder; fold in bread cubes and pineapple. Spread over fish. Cover and cook in 350° oven 20 minutes. Uncover and cook until fish flakes easily with fork, 15 to 20 minutes. Garnish with snipped parsley if desired.

4 to 6 servings.

COD AND VEGETABLE BAKE

2 pounds cod fillets
3 tablespoons lemon juice
1½ teaspoons salt
⅛ teaspoon pepper
2 carrots, coarsely shredded
1 large stalk celery, finely chopped
1 onion, chopped
5 slices bread, cubed
½ cup margarine or butter, melted
½ teaspoon salt
½ teaspoon ground sage
½ teaspoon ground thyme
3 tablespoons dry bread crumbs
2 tablespoons snipped parsley
½ teaspoon paprika

Cut fish into 6 serving pieces if necessary; place in ungreased 12x7½x2-inch or 8x8x2-inch baking dish. Sprinkle with lemon juice, 1½ teaspoons salt and the pepper.

Mix carrots, celery, onion, bread cubes, margarine, ½ teaspoon salt, the sage and thyme. Spread evenly over fish. Mix bread crumbs, parsley and paprika; sprinkle over vegetables. Cover and cook in 350° oven until fish flakes easily with fork, about 35 minutes.

6 servings.

SAUCY FISH BAKE

1 package (16 ounces) frozen fish
   fillets
½ teaspoon salt
⅛ teaspoon pepper
1 tablespoon margarine or butter
1 package (about 1⅛ ounces)
   Hollandaise sauce mix
1 can (16 ounces) whole green
   beans, drained
   Paprika
1 can (2.8 ounces) French fried
   onions

Thaw fish fillets just until they can be separated. Sprinkle both sides of fish with salt. Arrange fish in ungreased 11x7x1½-inch baking dish, leaving a space in center of dish. Sprinkle with pepper and dot with margarine. Cook uncovered in 375° oven 15 minutes.

Prepare sauce mix as directed on package. Remove fish from oven. Place beans in center of dish. Pour hot sauce over beans; sprinkle with paprika. Sprinkle onions over fish. Cook until fish flakes easily with fork and beans are hot, 5 to 7 minutes.

4 servings.

■ **To Microwave:** To thaw fish fillets, microwave in package on medium-low (30%) until fillets can be separated, 2 to 3 minutes. Let stand 5 minutes. Arrange beans in center and fish around edges of 11x7x1½-inch microwaveproof baking dish. Cover tightly and microwave on high (100%) until fish flakes easily with fork and beans are hot, 7 to 9 minutes.

Prepare sauce mix in 2-cup microwaveproof measure; microwave on medium (50%) until hot and thick, 2 to 3 minutes. Pour sauce over beans and sprinkle with paprika. Sprinkle onions over fish. Microwave uncovered on medium (50%) until onions are hot, 1 to 2 minutes.

Pictured at right: Three fish combos—Saucy Fish Bake (above) features crispy French fried onions, Crunchy Fish-Noodle Casserole (page 59) sports a colorful mandarin orange garnish, Tuna-Pasta Bake (page 62) has a golden cheese topping.

TUNA-RICE BAKE

1½ cups shredded process American cheese (about 6 ounces)
1 cup uncooked regular rice
½ cup water
⅓ cup sliced pimiento-stuffed olives
1 small onion, chopped (about ¼ cup)
1 can (13 ounces) evaporated milk
1 can (6½ ounces) tuna, drained
2 tablespoons snipped parsley
2 teaspoons dry mustard
1 teaspoon salt
Dash of pepper

Heat ¾ cup of the cheese and the remaining ingredients to boiling in 2-quart saucepan, stirring occasionally. Pour into ungreased 1½-quart casserole or 10x6x1½-inch baking dish. Sprinkle remaining cheese on top. Cover and cook in 350° oven until rice is tender and liquid is absorbed, 30 to 35 minutes.

6 servings.

■ To Microwave: Mix ¾ cup of the cheese, 1½ cups uncooked instant rice and the remaining ingredients in 2-quart microwaveproof casserole. Cover tightly and microwave on high (100%) 10 minutes; stir. Sprinkle remaining cheese on top. Cover and microwave until rice is tender and cheese is melted, 3 to 5 minutes longer.

CURRIED TUNA CASSEROLE

2 cans (6½ ounces each) tuna, drained
1 can (10¾ ounces) condensed cream of mushroom soup
1 can (8 ounces) small whole onions, drained and cut into halves
3 cups cooked rice
¾ cup milk
1½ teaspoons curry powder

OVEN METHOD: Mix all ingredients in ungreased 2-quart casserole or 12x7½x2-inch baking dish. Cook uncovered in 350° oven until hot and bubbly, 30 to 40 minutes.

RANGE-TOP METHOD: Mix all ingredients in 3-quart saucepan. Heat over medium heat, stirring occasionally, until hot, 8 to 10 minutes. Pour into serving dish.

Top with one or more of the following: sieved hard-cooked egg yolks, chopped peanuts, currants, crabapple jelly, sliced green onions and crumbled bacon.

6 servings.

■ To Microwave: Mix all ingredients in 2-quart microwaveproof casserole. Cover tightly and microwave on high (100%) 5 minutes; stir. Cover and microwave until hot and bubbly, 3 to 5 minutes longer. Top as directed above.

TUNA-PASTA BAKE

1 package (7 ounces) macaroni shells
1 medium onion, chopped (about ½ cup)
1 package (8 ounces) pasteurized process cheese spread
1 medium stalk celery, chopped (about ½ cup)
2 cans (6½ ounces each) tuna, drained
1 can (10¾ ounces) condensed cream of chicken or cream of shrimp soup
⅔ cup milk
1 jar (2 ounces) sliced pimiento, drained
1 teaspoon lemon juice

Cook macaroni as directed on package; drain. Spread in greased 2-quart casserole. Sprinkle with onion. Cut enough cheese into ½-inch cubes to measure 1 cup; reserve remaining cheese for topping. Mix cheese cubes and the remaining ingredients; stir into macaroni. Cover and cook in 375° oven 35 minutes. Cut reserved cheese into thin slices; place slices on macaroni mixture. Uncover and cook 5 minutes longer.

6 servings.

TUNA-MACARONI CASEROLE

1 cup uncooked elbow macaroni (about 3 ounces)
1 envelope (1 to 1½ ounces) white sauce mix
1 tablespoon peanut butter
2 cans (6½ ounces each) tuna, drained
1 can (4 ounces) mushroom stems and pieces
½ small green pepper, chopped (about ¼ cup)
½ cup sliced pitted ripe olives
1 to 1½ teaspoons seasoned salt
¼ teaspoon dried oregano leaves
¼ teaspoon pepper
1 cup shredded Cheddar or process American cheese (about 4 ounces)

Cook macaroni as directed on package; drain. Prepare 1 cup medium white sauce in 3-quart saucepan as directed on sauce mix package; stir in peanut butter. Stir in macaroni, tuna, mushrooms (with liquid), green pepper, olives, seasoned salt, oregano and pepper.

OVEN METHOD: Pour into ungreased 1½-quart casserole or 10x6x1½-inch baking dish. Sprinkle with cheese. Cook uncovered in 350° oven until hot and bubbly, about 30 minutes.

RANGE-TOP METHOD: Cover and heat, stirring occasionally, until tuna is hot, 8 to 10 minutes. Sprinkle with cheese. Cover and heat until cheese is melted, about 1 minute longer.

4 to 6 servings.

TUNA NOODLES ROMANOFF

4 cups uncooked egg noodles (about 8 ounces)
2 cans (6½ ounces each) tuna, well drained
1½ cups dairy sour cream
¾ cup milk
1 can (4 ounces) sliced mushrooms, drained
1½ teaspoons salt
¼ teaspoon pepper
¼ cup dry bread crumbs
¼ cup grated Parmesan cheese
2 tablespoons margarine or butter, melted
Paprika

Cook noodles as directed on package; drain. Mix noodles, tuna, sour cream, milk, mushrooms, salt and pepper in ungreased 2-quart casserole or 8x8x2-inch baking dish. Mix bread crumbs, cheese and margarine; sprinkle over top. Sprinkle with paprika. Cook uncovered in 350° oven until hot and bubbly, 35 to 40 minutes.

6 to 8 servings.

Salmon-Noodles Romanoff: Substitute 1 can (15½ ounces) salmon, drained and flaked, for the tuna.

Do-ahead Note: Before cooking, cover and refrigerate no longer than 24 hours. To serve, cook covered in 350° oven 40 minutes. Uncover and cook 10 minutes longer.

Measuring Up

The recipe you're using calls for cooked pasta and you're not sure where to start? Here's an easy-to-follow guide:

	Uncooked	Cooked
Macaroni	6 or 7 ounces or 2 cups	4 cups
Spaghetti	7 or 8 ounces	4 cups
Noodles	8 ounces or 4 to 5 cups	4 to 5 cups

TUNA-SPAGHETTI CASSEROLE

8 ounces uncooked spaghetti or linguine
1 can (10¾ ounces) condensed cream of mushroom soup
1 can (10¾ ounces) condensed cream of chicken soup
¾ cup milk
2 tablespoons dry white wine
1 can (4 ounces) mushroom stems and pieces, drained
1 can (9¼ ounces) tuna, drained
½ cup grated Parmesan cheese

Cook spaghetti as directed on package; drain. Mix mushroom soup, chicken soup, milk and wine in ungreased 8x8x2-inch pan. Stir in spaghetti, mushrooms and tuna. Sprinkle with cheese. Cook uncovered in 375° oven until hot and bubbly, about 30 minutes.

6 servings.

Do-ahead Note: Before cooking, wrap, label and freeze no longer than 2 months. To serve, cook uncovered in 425° oven until hot and bubbly, about 1½ hours.

Storing Cheese

All types of cheese—hard or soft, grated or whole—require refrigeration. Store soft cheese, such as cottage cheese and cream cheese, tightly covered. Cottage cheese will keep for 3 to 5 days; other soft cheeses will keep for up to 2 weeks. Hard cheese, such as Cheddar and Parmesan, will keep for several months. For best results, store unopened in original wrappers. If opened, wrap tightly with plastic wrap or aluminum foil.

To freeze cheese, overwrap the unopened package with freezer paper. Slices and loaves of natural cheese (such as Cheddar and Swiss) and pasteurized process cheese products can be frozen up to 3 months. To use, thaw frozen cheese in its wrapping in the refrigerator.

TUNA LASAGNE

9 uncooked lasagne noodles (about 8 ounces)
2 medium stalks celery, thinly sliced (about 1 cup)
1 medium green pepper, chopped (about 1 cup)
1 medium onion, chopped (about ½ cup)
1 clove garlic, chopped
⅓ cup margarine or butter
⅓ cup all-purpose flour
1 teaspoon salt
¼ teaspoon pepper
3 cups milk
1 can (6½ ounces) tuna, drained
¼ cup chopped pimiento
2 cups shredded Cheddar or process American cheese (about 8 ounces)
2 tablespoons margarine or butter, melted
¼ cup dry bread crumbs
¼ cup grated Parmesan cheese
½ teaspoon paprika

Cook noodles as directed on package; drain. Cook and stir celery, green pepper, onion and garlic in ⅓ cup margarine in 3-quart saucepan until crisp-tender. Stir in flour, salt and pepper; remove from heat. Stir in milk. Heat to boiling, stirring constantly. Boil and stir 1 minute. Stir in tuna and pimiento.

Layer ⅓ each of the noodles, Cheddar cheese and sauce in ungreased 13x9x2-inch baking pan; repeat 2 times. Mix 2 tablespoons margarine, the bread crumbs, Parmesan cheese and paprika; sprinkle over top. Cook uncovered in 350° oven until bubbly and light brown, 35 to 40 minutes. Let stand 10 minutes before cutting.

8 to 10 servings.

Do-ahead Note: Before cooking, cover and refrigerate no longer than 24 hours. To serve, cook uncovered in 350° oven 50 to 60 minutes.

TUNA-ASPARAGUS CASSEROLE

1 package (10 ounces) frozen cut
   asparagus, cooked and drained
1 can (10¾ ounces) condensed
   cream of chicken soup
½ cup dairy sour cream
1 can (4 ounces) mushroom stems
   and pieces
1 can (6½ ounces) tuna, drained
1 small green pepper, chopped
   (about ½ cup)
¼ cup slivered almonds
2 tablespoons chopped pimiento
2½ cups uncooked egg noodles
   (about 5 ounces)
1 cup shredded Cheddar or
   process American cheese
   (about 4 ounces)

Spread asparagus in ungreased 8x8x2- or 10x6x1½-inch baking dish. Mix soup, sour cream and mushrooms (with liquid). Stir in tuna, green pepper, almonds and pimiento. Fold in noodles. Spread over asparagus. Cover and cook in 350° oven until noodles are tender, 35 to 40 minutes. Sprinkle with cheese. Cook uncovered until cheese is melted, about 5 minutes.

6 servings.

Do-ahead Note: Before cooking, cover and refrigerate no longer than 24 hours. To serve, cook covered in 350° oven 50 to 55 minutes. Sprinkle with cheese. Cook uncovered until cheese is melted, about 5 minutes.

IMPOSSIBLE TUNA PIE

1 can (6½ ounces) tuna, drained
1 cup shredded process American
   cheese (about 4 ounces)
1 package (3 ounces) cream cheese,
   cut into about ¼-inch cubes
¼ cup thinly sliced green onions
2 cups milk
1 cup buttermilk baking mix
4 eggs
¾ teaspoon salt
   Dash of ground nutmeg

Heat oven to 400°. Lightly grease 10x1½-inch pie plate. Mix tuna, cheeses and onions in pie plate. Beat remaining ingredients until smooth, 15 seconds in blender on high speed or 1 minute with hand beater. Pour into pie plate. Bake until golden brown and knife inserted halfway between center and edge comes out clean, 35 to 40 minutes. Let stand 5 minutes before cutting. Refrigerate any remaining pie.

6 to 8 servings.

Impossible Crabmeat Pie: Substitute 1 can (6 ounces) crabmeat, drained and cartilage removed, for the tuna.

Impossible Shrimp Pie: Substitute 1 can (4¼ ounces) shrimp, rinsed and drained, for the tuna.

You can cook it in the microwave...   You can cook it on top of the range...   Or you can cook it in the oven...

Tuna Chow Mein Casserole (right)—an all-time favorite, now with a choice of preparation methods.

TUNA CHOW MEIN CASSEROLE

2 medium stalks celery, chopped (about 1 cup)
1 small onion, chopped (about ¼ cup)
2 tablespoons chopped green pepper
1 tablespoon margarine or butter
1 can (3 ounces) chow mein noodles (about 1⅓ cups)
1 can (10¾ ounces) condensed cream of mushroom soup
1 can (6½ ounces) tuna, drained
½ cup water
⅛ teaspoon pepper
¾ cup salted cashews or peanuts

Cook and stir celery, onion and green pepper in margarine in 10-inch skillet until onion is tender. Reserve ⅓ cup of the noodles. Stir in remaining noodles and the remaining ingredients.

OVEN METHOD: Pour into ungreased 1½-quart casserole; sprinkle with reserved noodles. Cook uncovered in 350° oven until hot and bubbly, about 30 minutes.

RANGE-TOP METHOD: Heat to boiling; reduce heat. Cover and simmer, stirring occasionally, until celery is tender, about 10 minutes. Sprinkle with reserved noodles.

5 or 6 servings.

■ To Microwave: Microwave margarine in 1½-quart microwaveproof casserole on high (100%) until melted, 30 to 45 seconds. Stir in celery, onion and green pepper. Cover and microwave until tender, 2 to 3 minutes. Continue as directed. Microwave uncovered until hot and bubbly, 5 to 7 minutes. Sprinkle with reserved noodles.

TUNA-CRACKER CASSEROLE

1 can (10½ ounces) condensed chicken with rice soup
1 can (10¾ ounces) condensed cream of mushroom soup
2 cans (6½ ounces each) tuna, drained
1 can (4 ounces) mushroom stems and pieces, drained
1 jar (2 ounces) diced pimiento
1 small green pepper, chopped
1 small onion, chopped (about ¼ cup)
¼ teaspoon pepper
¼ cup toasted chopped almonds
3 cups oyster crackers

Mix soups in greased 2-quart casserole or 12x7½x2-inch baking dish. Stir in remaining ingredients. Cook uncovered in 350° oven until hot and bubbly, 30 to 35 minutes.

6 to 8 servings.

■ To Microwave: Place green pepper and onion in 12x7½x2-inch microwaveproof baking dish. Cover tightly and microwave on high (100%) until tender, 1 to 3 minutes. Stir in remaining ingredients. Cover tightly and microwave until hot, 8 to 10 minutes.

TUNA AND CHIPS

1 can (10¾ ounces) condensed cream of mushroom soup
½ cup milk
1 can (6½ ounces) tuna, drained
1¼ cups crushed potato chips
1 cup cooked green peas

Mix soup and milk in ungreased 1-quart casserole. Stir in tuna, 1 cup of the chips and the peas. Sprinkle with remaining chips. Cook uncovered in 350° oven until hot, about 25 minutes.

4 servings.

■ To Microwave: Mix ingredients as directed in 1-quart microwaveproof casserole except— do not sprinkle remaining chips over casserole. Microwave uncovered on high (100%) 5 minutes; sprinkle remaining chips over casserole. Microwave until hot, about 4 minutes.

CRUNCHY TUNA CASSEROLE

1 can (16 ounces) cut green beans
1 can (10¾ ounces) condensed
    cream of mushroom soup
1 can (2.8 ounces) French fried
    onions
2 cans (6½ ounces each) tuna, drained
1 cup thinly sliced celery
2 tablespoons chopped pimiento
1 tablespoon soy sauce

Drain green beans, reserving ¼ cup liquid. Mix soup and reserved bean liquid. Fold half of the onions and the remaining ingredients into soup mixture. Pour into ungreased 2-quart casserole or 12x7½x2-inch baking dish. Cover and cook in 350° oven 30 minutes. Sprinkle with remaining onions; cook uncovered 5 minutes longer.

6 servings.

■ **To Microwave:** Pour into 2-quart microwaveproof casserole. Cover tightly and microwave on high (100%) until hot, 5 to 7 minutes; stir. Sprinkle with remaining onions. Microwave uncovered 2 minutes longer.

TUNA-POTATO PUFF

Instant mashed potatoes for
    4 servings
2 eggs, beaten
1 teaspoon salt
4 or 5 drops red pepper sauce
1 package (9 ounces) frozen cut
    green beans, thawed and drained
1 can (6½ ounces) tuna, drained
1 medium onion, chopped (about
    ½ cup)

Prepare mashed potatoes as directed on package except—omit salt. Gradually stir in eggs, salt and pepper sauce. Fold in remaining ingredients. Pour into ungreased 1-quart casserole. Cook uncovered in 375° oven until golden brown, 40 to 45 minutes.

4 servings.

Do-ahead Note: Before cooking, cover and refrigerate no longer than 24 hours. To serve, cook uncovered in 375° oven 55 to 60 minutes.

TUNA-POTATO SCALLOP

¼ cup margarine or butter
¼ cup all-purpose flour
¼ teaspoon salt
    Dash of pepper
½ teaspoon dry mustard
1 cup milk
1 cup shredded process American or
    Cheddar cheese (about 4 ounces)
1 medium onion, chopped (about ½
    cup)
¼ cup snipped parsley
2 cups thinly sliced cooked potatoes
1 can (6½ ounces) tuna, drained
¼ cup dry bread crumbs
2 tablespoons margarine or butter,
    melted

Heat ¼ cup margarine in 2-quart saucepan over low heat until melted. Stir in flour, salt, pepper and mustard. Cook over low heat, stirring constantly, until smooth and bubbly. Stir in milk. Heat to boiling, stirring constantly. Boil and stir 1 minute. Stir in cheese, onion and parsley.

OVEN METHOD: Layer potatoes, tuna and sauce in greased 1½-quart casserole or 10x6x 1½-inch baking dish. Mix bread crumbs and 2 tablespoons margarine; sprinkle over top. Cook uncovered in 375° oven until bubbly and golden brown, 40 to 45 minutes.

RANGE-TOP METHOD: Mix in potatoes and tuna. Heat over medium heat, stirring occasionally, until potatoes are hot. Cook and stir bread crumbs and 2 tablespoons margarine in skillet until golden brown; sprinkle over top.

4 to 6 servings.

Do-ahead Note: Prepare as directed for Oven Method except—before cooking, cover and refrigerate no longer than 24 hours. To serve, cook covered in 375° oven 30 minutes. Uncover and cook 20 to 30 minutes longer.

SALMON SOUFFLE

½ cup milk
2 tablespoons margarine or butter, melted
4 slices bread, torn into pieces
1 can (15½ ounces) salmon, drained and flaked
2 eggs, separated
3 tablespoons lemon juice
2 teaspoons finely chopped onion
1 teaspoon salt
½ teaspoon pepper
   Paprika

Mix milk, margarine and bread; stir in salmon, egg yolks, lemon juice, onion, salt and pepper. Beat egg whites in large bowl until stiff; fold in salmon mixture. Pour into greased 1½-quart casserole. Sprinkle with paprika. Cook uncovered in 350° oven until puffed and golden, about 1 hour.

6 servings.

Tuna Soufflé: Substitute 2 cans (6½ ounces each) tuna, drained, for the salmon.

SALMON-POTATO CASSEROLE

1 can (15½ ounces) salmon, drained (reserve liquid)
1 can (10¾ ounces) condensed cream of mushroom soup
½ cup dairy sour cream
1 teaspoon salt
¼ teaspoon dill weed
1 package (10 ounces) frozen green peas
1 package (16 ounces) frozen French fries
2 medium stalks celery, thinly sliced (about 1 cup)

Mix reserved salmon liquid, the soup, sour cream, salt and dill weed. Rinse frozen peas under running cold water to separate; drain. Layer half each of the French fries, salmon, peas, celery and soup mixture in ungreased 2-quart casserole or 8x8x2-inch baking dish; repeat. Cook uncovered in 350° oven until hot and bubbly, about 1 hour. Sprinkle with paprika if desired.

7 or 8 servings.

French fries are the surprise layer in Salmon-Potato Casserole.

SALMON 'N SPAGHETTI

1⅓ cups uncooked elbow spaghetti
     or macaroni (about 4 ounces)
  1 medium onion, chopped (about
     ½ cup)
  ¼ cup margarine or butter
  2 tablespoons all-purpose flour
  1 can (15½ ounces) salmon,
     drained (reserve liquid)
1¾ cups milk
  ½ teaspoon salt
  ⅛ teaspoon paprika
  1 tablespoon lemon juice
  ¼ cup snipped parsley
  1 cup shredded Cheddar cheese
     (about 4 ounces)

Cook spaghetti as directed on package; drain. Cook and stir onion in margarine until tender. Blend in flour. Cook over low heat, stirring constantly, until smooth and bubbly; remove from heat. Stir in reserved salmon liquid and the milk. Cook over low heat, stirring constantly, until slightly thickened; remove from heat. Stir in salt, paprika, lemon juice and parsley.

OVEN METHOD: Layer spaghetti, salmon (broken apart) and ¾ cup of the cheese in ungreased 2-quart casserole or 8x8x2-inch baking dish. Pour sauce over top; sprinkle with remaining cheese. Cook uncovered in 375° oven until bubbly and cheese is light brown, 20 to 25 minutes.

RANGE-TOP METHOD: Stir in spaghetti, salmon and ¾ cup of the cheese. Cover and heat over medium heat, stirring occasionally, until hot, about 10 minutes. Sprinkle with remaining cheese. Cover and heat until cheese is melted, about 2 minutes longer.

6 to 8 servings.

Tuna 'n Spaghetti: Substitute 2 cans (6½ ounces each) tuna, drained, for the salmon. Increase milk to 2 cups.

Do-ahead Note: Prepare as directed for Oven Method except—before cooking, cover and refrigerate no longer than 24 hours. To serve, cook covered in 350° oven 30 minutes. Uncover and cook 10 minutes longer.

CURRIED SHRIMP CASSEROLE

  1 cup uncooked elbow macaroni
     (about 3 ounces)
  1 can (10¾ ounces) condensed
     cream of shrimp soup
  ¾ cup milk
  2 tablespoons snipped parsley
  ½ to 1 teaspoon curry powder
  2 cups cleaned cooked shrimp
  1 cup soft bread crumbs
  2 tablespoons margarine or butter,
     melted

Cook macaroni as directed on package; drain. Heat soup, milk, parsley and curry powder to boiling, stirring occasionally. Stir in shrimp and macaroni.

OVEN METHOD: Pour into greased 1½-quart casserole or 10x6x1½-inch baking dish. Mix bread crumbs and margarine; sprinkle over top. Cook uncovered in 375° oven until hot and bubbly, about 30 minutes.

RANGE-TOP METHOD: Heat to boiling; reduce heat. Cover and simmer, stirring occasionally, until shrimp is hot, about 5 minutes. Mix bread crumbs and margarine; sprinkle over top.

4 servings.

■ **To Microwave:** Cook macaroni as directed on package; drain. Heat margarine on high (100%) until melted. Mix in bread crumbs. Microwave uncovered until crisp and golden, about 2 minutes. Stir once or twice. Mix soup, milk, parsley and curry powder in 1½-quart microwaveproof casserole. Microwave uncovered on high (100%) until hot, 3 to 4 minutes. Stir in shrimp and macaroni. Microwave uncovered until shrimp is hot, 3 to 4 minutes. Sprinkle with bread crumbs.

BAKED CRAB AND SHRIMP

1 medium green pepper, chopped
   (about 1 cup)
1 medium onion, chopped (about ½
   cup)
2 medium stalks celery, chopped
   (about 1 cup)
1 can (6½ ounces) crabmeat,
   drained and cartilage removed
1 can (4¼ ounces) shrimp, rinsed
   and drained
1 teaspoon Worcestershire sauce
½ teaspoon salt
⅛ teaspoon pepper
1 cup mayonnaise or salad dressing
⅓ cup dry bread crumbs
2 tablespoons margarine or butter,
   melted

Mix all ingredients except bread crumbs and margarine. Pour into ungreased 1-quart casserole or 6 individual baking shells. Mix bread crumbs and margarine; sprinkle over top. Cook uncovered in 350° oven 30 minutes.

6 servings.

■ **To Microwave:** Heat margarine on high (100%) until melted. Mix in bread crumbs. Microwave uncovered until crisp and golden brown, about 2 minutes. Stir once or twice. Place green pepper, onion and celery in 1-quart microwaveproof casserole. Microwave uncovered on high (100%) until crisp-tender, 2 to 3 minutes. Stir in seafood, Worcestershire sauce, salt, pepper and mayonnaise. Microwave uncovered on medium-high (70%) until hot, 6 to 8 minutes. Sprinkle with bread crumbs.

CRAB PUFF

1 can (6½ ounces) crabmeat,
   drained and cartilage removed
½ cup chopped celery
1 small green pepper, chopped
1 medium onion, chopped (about
   ½ cup)
⅓ cup mayonnaise or salad dressing
¾ teaspoon salt
½ teaspoon dry mustard
6 slices bread
4 eggs, beaten
2 cups milk
1 cup shredded Cheddar cheese
   (about 4 ounces)
   Paprika

Mix crabmeat, celery, green pepper, onion, mayonnaise, salt and mustard. Remove crusts from bread. Cut bread into cubes. Spread cubes in ungreased 8x8x2-inch baking dish. Spread crabmeat mixture over bread. Mix eggs and milk; pour over top. Sprinkle with cheese and paprika. Cook uncovered in 325° oven until knife inserted in center comes out clean, 55 to 60 minutes. Let stand 10 minutes before cutting.

9 servings.

Shrimp Puff: Substitute 1 can (4¼ ounces) shrimp, rinsed and drained, for the crabmeat.

For Crumbs and Croutons

Bread crumbs (both dry and soft) and croutons are called for in many casserole recipes. You can avoid the pricey packaged varieties and make them yourself in no time.

Soft Crumbs: Tear day-old bread into small pieces with fingers or a fork.

Dry Crumbs: Dry bread in slow oven until dry but not brown. Then crush with a rolling pin or process in a blender or food processor according to the manufacturer's directions.

Croutons: Trim crust from bread; cut bread into ½-inch cubes. Toast in 300° oven, stirring occasionally, until crisp and golden brown. Toss with melted margarine or butter.

SPINACH NOODLE-CRAB CASSEROLE

2½ cups uncooked green spinach
      noodles (about 4 ounces)
  1 small onion, finely chopped
      (about ¼ cup)
  2 tablespoons margarine or butter
  2 tablespoons all-purpose flour
 ½ teaspoon salt
 ¼ teaspoon pepper
 ¼ teaspoon dry mustard
1½ cups milk
  1 cup shredded process American
      cheese (about 4 ounces)
 ¼ cup dry white wine
  2 cans (6½ ounces each) crabmeat,
      drained and cartilage removed,
      or 12 ounces frozen cooked
      crabmeat, thawed
  2 tablespoons lemon juice
 ½ cup shredded process American
      cheese

Cook noodles as directed on package; drain. Cook and stir onion in margarine until tender. Stir in flour, salt, pepper and mustard. Cook over low heat, stirring constantly, until smooth and bubbly. Stir in milk. Heat to boiling, stirring constantly. Boil and stir 1 minute. Stir in 1 cup cheese until melted. Stir in wine.

Arrange noodles around sides of ungreased 10x6x1½-inch baking dish. Place crabmeat in center; sprinkle with lemon juice. Pour sauce over noodles and crabmeat; sprinkle with ½ cup cheese. Cook uncovered in 375° oven until bubbly and light brown, about 25 minutes.

5 servings.

Spinach Noodle-Seafood Casserole: Substitute 1½ cups bite-size pieces cooked fish (flounder, haddock, halibut, sole or other fish fillets) or cubed cooked lobster meat for the crabmeat.

Spinach Noodle-Crab Casserole—perfect for a special occasion.

DIXIE CRAB BAKE

¼ cup margarine or butter
2 tablespoons all-purpose flour
1 cup half-and-half
1 teaspoon prepared mustard
½ teaspoon salt
¼ teaspoon pepper
¼ teaspoon ground mace
1 tablespoon lemon juice
1 cup cooked sliced carrots
2 cans (6½ ounces each) crabmeat, drained and cartilage removed
2 hard-cooked eggs, finely chopped
½ cup soft bread crumbs
2 tablespoons margarine or butter, melted

Heat ¼ cup margarine in 2-quart saucepan over low heat until melted. Stir in flour. Cook, stirring constantly, until smooth and bubbly; remove from heat. Stir in half-and-half. Heat to boiling, stirring constantly. Boil and stir 1 minute; reduce heat. Fold in seasonings, lemon juice, carrots, crabmeat and eggs.

OVEN METHOD: Pour into ungreased 1½-quart casserole or 10x6x1½-inch baking dish. Mix bread crumbs and 2 tablespoons margarine; sprinkle over top. Cook uncovered in 350° oven until hot, about 45 minutes.

RANGE-TOP METHOD: Cover and heat, stirring occasionally, until hot, about 5 minutes. Cook and stir bread crumbs and 2 tablespoons margarine until crumbs are lightly toasted; sprinkle over top.

4 to 6 servings.

OYSTERS AND NOODLES DELUXE

3 cups uncooked egg noodles (about 6 ounces)
Milk
2 cans (8 ounces each) oysters, drained (reserve liquor)
½ cup margarine or butter, softened
1 egg
1 tablespoon all-purpose flour
1 clove garlic, crushed
½ teaspoon bottled browning sauce
¼ teaspoon ground mace
Dash of cayenne pepper
1¾ cups shredded process sharp American cheese (about 7 ounces)
3 tablespoons snipped parsley
¼ teaspoon freshly ground black pepper
¼ cup shredded process sharp American cheese
¼ cup dry bread crumbs
2 tablespoons margarine or butter, melted

Cook noodles as directed on package; drain. Add enough milk to reserved oyster liquor to measure 2 cups. Heat oysters and milk-liquor mixture in 10-inch skillet over medium heat 5 minutes. Mix ½ cup margarine, the egg, flour, garlic, browning sauce, mace and cayenne pepper; gradually stir into oyster mixture. Heat to boiling over medium heat, stirring constantly. Boil and stir 1 minute. Stir in noodles, 1¾ cups cheese, the parsley and pepper.

Pour into ungreased 2-quart casserole or 8x8x2-inch baking dish. Mix ¼ cup cheese, the bread crumbs and 2 tablespoons margarine; sprinkle over top. Cook uncovered in 350° oven until bubbly and light brown, about 20 minutes.

6 servings.

Do-ahead Note: Before cooking, cover and refrigerate no longer than 24 hours. To serve, cook covered in 350° oven 30 minutes. Uncover and cook 10 minutes longer.

CLAM SPAGHETTI

1 package (7 ounces) elbow
    spaghetti
1 clove garlic, chopped
¼ cup margarine or butter
1 can (6 ounces) minced clams
2 tablespoons chopped pimiento
2 tablespoons snipped parsley
½ cup grated Parmesan cheese

Cook spaghetti as directed on package; drain. Cook and stir garlic in margarine in 2-quart saucepan until light brown. Stir in spaghetti, clams (with liquor), the pimiento, parsley and half of the cheese.

OVEN METHOD: Pour into ungreased 1-quart casserole. Sprinkle with remaining cheese. Cook uncovered in 350° oven until hot, 15 to 20 minutes.

RANGE-TOP METHOD: Heat to boiling; reduce heat. Simmer uncovered until hot, 2 to 3 minutes. Sprinkle with remaining cheese.

4 servings.

Oyster Spaghetti: Substitute 1 can (8 ounces) oysters, drained and finely chopped, for the clams.

CLAM SQUARES WITH SHRIMP SAUCE

3 cups cooked rice
1 small onion, chopped (about
    ¼ cup)
¼ cup snipped parsley
1 jar (2 ounces) diced pimiento,
    drained
1 cup shredded sharp Cheddar
    cheese (about 4 ounces)
1 teaspoon salt
1 teaspoon Worcestershire sauce
1 can (6 ounces) minced clams,
    drained
3 eggs, slightly beaten
2 cups milk
    Shrimp Sauce (below)

Mix all ingredients except Shrimp Sauce in ungreased 13x9x2-inch baking dish. Cook uncovered in 325° oven until knife inserted in center comes out clean, about 45 minutes. Cut into squares; serve with Shrimp Sauce.

6 to 8 servings.

SHRIMP SAUCE

1 can (10¾ ounces) condensed
    cream of shrimp soup
½ cup dairy sour cream
1 teaspoon lemon juice
¼ teaspoon salt

Heat all ingredients over medium heat, stirring constantly, until hot.

Do-ahead Note: Before cooking, cover and refrigerate no longer than 24 hours. To serve, cook uncovered in 325° oven 50 to 60 minutes. Serve with Shrimp Sauce.

Egg, Cheese & Bean Casseroles

CHEESY EGGS AND MUSHROOMS

    8 ounces mushrooms, sliced
    2 slices bacon, diced
    ½ cup sliced green onions
   12 eggs, beaten
    2 tablespoons margarine or butter
    2 tablespoons all-purpose flour
    1 teaspoon dry mustard
    ¾ teaspoon salt
    ⅛ teaspoon pepper
    2 cups milk
    1 cup shredded sharp Cheddar
        cheese (about 4 ounces)

Cook and stir mushrooms, bacon and onions over low heat until bacon is crisp; drain. Stir in eggs. Pour into ungreased 12x7½x2-inch baking dish.

Heat margarine in 2-quart saucepan over low heat until melted. Stir in flour, mustard, salt and pepper. Cook, stirring constantly, until smooth and bubbly; remove from heat. Stir in milk. Heat to boiling, stirring constantly. Boil and stir 1 minute. Stir in cheese. Heat over low heat, stirring constantly, until cheese is melted. Pour over egg mixture. Cook uncovered in 350° oven until center is set and top is golden brown, about 30 minutes.

8 servings.

WESTERN CASSEROLE

    2 tablespoons margarine or butter
    ¾ cup dry bread crumbs
    1 medium onion, chopped
    1 small green pepper, chopped
    1 cup finely chopped fully cooked
        smoked ham
    3 tablespoons vegetable oil
    8 eggs
    ½ cup milk
    1 teaspoon Worcestershire sauce
    ½ teaspoon salt
    ⅛ teaspoon pepper
    ½ cup shredded Cheddar cheese

Heat margarine in 10-inch skillet over medium heat until melted. Add bread crumbs; cook and stir until light brown. Reserve 2 tablespoons of the crumbs; spread remaining crumbs in ungreased 1½-quart casserole. Cook and stir onion, green pepper and ham in oil until onion is tender. Beat eggs, milk, Worcestershire sauce, salt and pepper with hand beater. Pour egg mixture over ham mixture in skillet. Cook over low heat, stirring gently. Before eggs are completely set, quickly spoon into casserole. Sprinkle with cheese and reserved bread crumbs. Cook uncovered in 350° oven until eggs are desired consistency, about 15 minutes.

6 servings.

CHEESE 'N CHILIES OVEN OMELET

2 cups shredded Cheddar cheese (about 8 ounces)
1 can (4 ounces) chopped green chilies, drained
2 cups shredded Monterey Jack cheese (about 8 ounces)
1¼ cups milk
3 tablespoons all-purpose flour
½ teaspoon salt
3 eggs
1 can (8 ounces) tomato sauce

Layer Cheddar cheese, chilies and Monterey Jack cheese in lightly greased 8x8x2-inch baking dish. Beat milk, flour, salt and eggs; pour over cheese. Cook uncovered in 350° oven until center is set and top is golden brown, about 40 minutes. Let stand 10 minutes before cutting. Heat tomato sauce; serve with omelet.

8 servings.

OVEN OMELET

12 eggs
¾ cup dairy sour cream
1 teaspoon salt
2 small tomatoes, peeled and cut into ½-inch pieces (about 1 cup)
2 green onions, sliced
1½ cups shredded Cheddar or Swiss cheese (about 6 ounces)

Beat eggs, sour cream and salt in 2½-quart bowl on medium speed until well blended, about 1 minute. Stir in remaining ingredients. Pour into buttered 2-quart casserole. Cook uncovered in 325° oven until center is set and top is golden brown, 35 to 40 minutes.

9 servings.

SPINACH OVEN OMELET

9 eggs
1 package (10 ounces) frozen chopped spinach, thawed and drained
2 tablespoons finely chopped onion
2 tablespoons milk
1 teaspoon salt
½ teaspoon basil leaves
¼ teaspoon garlic powder
8 tomato slices
1 cup shredded mozzarella cheese (about 4 ounces)

Beat eggs until light and fluffy. Stir in spinach, onion, milk, salt, basil and garlic powder. Pour into greased 11x7x1½-inch baking dish. Arrange tomato slices on top; sprinkle with cheese. Cook uncovered in 350° oven until set, 25 to 30 minutes.

8 servings.

EGG AND RICE CASSEROLE

3 cups hot cooked rice
2 cups shredded Colby cheese (about 8 ounces)
1 package (10 ounces) frozen green peas, thawed
1 jar (2 ounces) diced pimiento, drained
¼ cup sliced green onions (with tops)
1½ teaspoons salt
½ teaspoon dried dill weed
4 eggs, beaten
1½ cups milk

Mix rice, cheese, peas, pimiento, onions, salt and dill weed. Spread in greased 12x7½x2-inch baking dish. Mix eggs and milk; pour over rice mixture. Cook uncovered in 350° oven until set, about 45 minutes.

8 servings.

Do-ahead Note: Before cooking, cover and refrigerate no longer than 24 hours. To serve, cook uncovered in 350° oven about 1 hour.

IMPOSSIBLE CHILIES-CHEESE PIE

2 cans (4 ounces each) chopped
   green chilies, drained
4 cups shredded Cheddar cheese
   (about 16 ounces)
2 cups milk
1 cup buttermilk baking mix
4 eggs

Heat oven to 425°. Grease 10x1½-inch pie plate. Sprinkle chilies and cheese in pie plate. Beat remaining ingredients until smooth, 15 seconds in blender on high speed or 1 minute with hand beater. Pour into pie plate. Bake until knife inserted between center and edge comes out clean, 25 to 30 minutes. Let stand 10 minutes before cutting. Serve with sour cream and guacamole if desired. Refrigerate any remaining pie.

6 to 8 servings.

EGG AND WILD RICE CASSEROLE

3 cups cooked wild rice
6 hard-cooked eggs, chopped
1 can (10¾ ounces) condensed
   cream of chicken soup
⅓ cup milk
1 can (8 ounces) sliced water
   chestnuts, drained
1 jar (4½ ounces) sliced mushrooms,
   drained
½ cup sliced green onions (with
   tops)
1 jar (2 ounces) diced pimiento,
   drained

Mix all ingredients in ungreased 1½-quart casserole or 10x6x1½-inch baking dish. Cook uncovered in 350° oven until hot and bubbly, about 40 minutes. Serve with soy sauce and lime wedges if desired.

4 servings.

Impossible Chilies-Cheese Pie is as easy as it is delicious.

CONFETTI RICE CASSEROLE

8 ounces process sharp American or Swiss cheese or process cheese spread loaf, cut into ½-inch cubes
⅓ cup milk
4 hard-cooked eggs, sliced
3 cups cooked rice
1 package (10 ounces) frozen mixed vegetables, thawed
1 medium onion, chopped (about ½ cup)
1 teaspoon salt

Heat cheese and milk in 3-quart saucepan over low heat, stirring constantly, until cheese is melted, about 5 minutes. Reserve 3 to 5 egg slices. Stir remaining egg slices and the remaining ingredients into cheese sauce. Pour into ungreased 1½-quart casserole or 10x6x1½-inch baking dish. Cook uncovered in 350° oven until hot and bubbly, 25 to 30 minutes. Garnish with reserved egg slices and, if desired, parsley.

6 servings.

EGGS AND CHIPS

2 cups crushed potato chips
6 hard-cooked eggs, sliced
¼ teaspoon salt
⅛ teaspoon pepper
1 can (10¾ ounces) condensed cream of celery soup
½ cup milk
2 tablespoons finely chopped onion
1 teaspoon prepared mustard

Place 1 cup of the chips in greased 1½-quart casserole or 10x6x1½-inch baking dish. Top with eggs; sprinkle with salt and pepper. Mix soup, milk, onion and mustard; pour over eggs. Sprinkle with remaining chips. Cook uncovered in 400° oven until hot and bubbly, about 25 minutes.

6 servings.

■ **To Microwave:** Prepare as directed in 1½-quart microwaveproof casserole. Microwave uncovered on high (100%) until hot, 7 to 10 minutes.

EGGS AU GRATIN CASSEROLE

¼ cup margarine or butter
⅓ cup all-purpose flour
2 cups hot water
1 cup milk
2 teaspoons instant chicken bouillon
1 cup shredded Cheddar cheese (about 4 ounces)
¾ teaspoon salt
½ teaspoon Worcestershire sauce
¼ teaspoon pepper
12 hard-cooked eggs, cut lengthwise into halves
⅓ to ½ cup grated Parmesan cheese
⅓ cup dry bread crumbs
2 tablespoons margarine or butter, melted

Heat ¼ cup margarine in 2-quart saucepan over low heat until melted. Stir in flour. Cook, stirring constantly, until smooth and bubbly; remove from heat. Stir in water, milk and instant bouillon. Heat to boiling, stirring constantly. Boil and stir 1 minute. Add Cheddar cheese, salt, Worcestershire sauce and pepper. Cook, stirring constantly, until cheese is melted.

Arrange eggs, cut sides up, in ungreased 13x9x2-inch baking dish; top with cheese sauce. Mix Parmesan cheese, bread crumbs and 2 tablespoons margarine; sprinkle over top. Cook uncovered in 350° oven until hot and topping is brown, 20 to 25 minutes.

6 to 8 servings.

Do-ahead Note: After sprinkling with bread crumb mixture, cover and refrigerate no longer than 8 hours. To serve, cook uncovered in 350° oven 35 to 40 minutes.

CHEESE-EGG BAKE

1 cup sliced onion
1 tablespoon margarine or butter
8 hard-cooked eggs, sliced
2 cups shredded Swiss cheese
    (about 8 ounces)
1 can (10¾ ounces) condensed
    cream of mushroom soup
¾ cup milk
1 teaspoon prepared mustard
½ teaspoon seasoned salt
¼ teaspoon dried dill weed
¼ teaspoon pepper
6 slices caraway rye bread, each
    buttered and cut diagonally into
    4 pieces

Cook and stir onion in margarine until tender. Spread in ungreased 11x7x1½-inch baking dish. Top with egg slices; sprinkle with cheese. Beat remaining ingredients except bread with hand beater; pour over cheese. Overlap bread on top. Cook uncovered in 350° oven until hot, 30 to 35 minutes. Set oven control to broil and/or 550°. Broil casserole with top about 5 inches from heat until bread is toasted, about 1 minute.

6 servings.

Hard-Cooking Eggs?

So you hard-cook eggs just the way your mother did. Did she know there were two methods?

Cold Water Method: Place eggs in saucepan; add enough cold water to come at least 1 inch above eggs. Heat rapidly to boiling; remove from heat. Cover and let stand 22 to 24 minutes. Immediately cool eggs in cold water to prevent further cooking.

Boiling Water Method: Place eggs in bowl of warm water to prevent shells from cracking. Fill saucepan with enough water to come at least 1 inch above eggs; heat to boiling. Transfer eggs from warm water to boiling water with spoon; reduce heat to below simmering. Cook uncovered 20 minutes. Immediately cool eggs in cold water to prevent further cooking.

CHILI-ZUCCHINI CASSEROLE

8 ounces Monterey Jack cheese, cut
    into ⅛-inch slices
3 cups cooked rice
2 medium zucchini, sliced
¾ cup chopped tomato
1 cup dairy sour cream
1 can (4 ounces) chopped green
    chilies, drained
1 small onion, chopped
½ teaspoon garlic salt
1 medium tomato, sliced

Reserve ¼ of the cheese slices. Layer half each of the rice, remaining cheese slices, zucchini and chopped tomato in ungreased 2-quart casserole or 12x7½x2-inch baking dish; repeat. Mix sour cream, chilies, onion and garlic salt; spread over chopped tomato. Arrange tomato slices on sour cream mixture; top with reserved cheese slices. Cook uncovered in 350° oven until hot, 45 to 50 minutes.

6 servings.

Do-ahead Note: Before cooking, cover and refrigerate no longer than 24 hours. To serve, cook uncovered in 350° oven 60 to 70 minutes.

BROCCOLI-CHEESE BAKE

2 cups milk
2 cups shredded process American
    cheese (about 8 ounces)
1 teaspoon dried marjoram leaves
1 teaspoon celery salt
1 teaspoon dried sage leaves
½ teaspoon salt
4 eggs
2½ cups plain croutons
1 package (10 ounces) frozen
    chopped broccoli, thawed

Heat milk, cheese, marjoram, celery salt, sage and salt, stirring constantly, until cheese is melted. Beat eggs; stir hot mixture slowly into eggs. Stir in croutons and broccoli. Pour into ungreased 1½-quart casserole or 10x6x1½-inch baking dish. Cook uncovered in 350° oven until center is set, 45 to 50 minutes.

6 servings.

THREE-CHEESE MEDLEY

1 cup shredded Monterey Jack
   cheese (about 4 ounces)
1 cup shredded Cheddar cheese
   (about 4 ounces)
¾ cup mayonnaise or salad dressing
½ cup sliced green onions (with tops)
1 can (8 ounces) sliced water
   chestnuts, drained
1 jar (2 ounces) diced pimiento,
   drained
4 cups hot cooked rice
½ cup grated Parmesan cheese

Mix Monterey Jack cheese, Cheddar cheese, mayonnaise, onions, water chestnuts and pimiento. Layer 2 cups of the rice and half of the cheese mixture in greased 2-quart casserole; repeat. Sprinkle with Parmesan cheese. Cook uncovered in 325° oven until hot, about 35 minutes.

6 servings.

DOUBLE CHEESE STRATA

2 tablespoons margarine or butter,
   softened
6 slices whole wheat bread
1 cup shredded Monterey Jack
   cheese (about 4 ounces)
1 cup shredded Gouda cheese
   (about 4 ounces)
¼ cup finely chopped onion
1 large clove garlic, crushed
1 teaspoon dry mustard
½ teaspoon salt
4 eggs, slightly beaten
1½ cups milk
½ cup dry white wine
¼ teaspoon red pepper sauce

Spread margarine on one side of each slice of bread. Cut each slice diagonally into 4 triangles. Place buttered sides of 8 triangles against sides of ungreased 8x8x2-inch baking dish. Place 8 triangles, buttered sides down, on bottom of dish.

Mix cheeses, onion, garlic, mustard and salt; spread over bread. Arrange remaining triangles, buttered sides up, on cheese mixture. Mix remaining ingredients. Pour over bread.

Cook uncovered in 325° oven until knife inserted in center comes out clean, about 1 hour 10 minutes. Let stand about 10 minutes before cutting.

6 servings.

SPANISH STRATA

6 slices white bread (crusts
   removed)
2 cups shredded Cheddar cheese
   (about 8 ounces)
¼ cup finely chopped onion
1 teaspoon salt
½ teaspoon Worcestershire sauce
   Dash of cayenne pepper
4 eggs
2½ cups milk
1 can (16 ounces) stewed tomatoes
1 tablespoon cornstarch
2 tablespoons cold water

Cut bread into 1-inch pieces. Place half of the bread in ungreased 8x8x2-inch baking dish. Mix cheese, onion, salt, Worcestershire sauce and cayenne pepper; spread over bread in dish. Top with remaining bread. Beat eggs and milk. Pour over bread. Cover and refrigerate at least 2 hours.

Cook uncovered in 325° oven until knife inserted in center comes out clean, about 1¼ hours. Let stand 10 minutes before cutting. Heat tomatoes to boiling. Mix cornstarch and water; stir into tomatoes. Boil and stir 1 minute. Serve with strata.

6 servings.

Do-ahead Note: Before cooking, cover and refrigerate no longer than 24 hours. To serve, cook uncovered in 325° oven 1¼ hours.

CHEESE STRATA

⅓ cup margarine or butter,
    softened
1 clove garlic, crushed
½ teaspoon dry mustard
10 slices white bread (crusts
    removed)
2 cups shredded sharp Cheddar
    cheese (about 8 ounces)
2 tablespoons chopped onion
2 tablespoons snipped parsley
1 teaspoon salt
½ teaspoon Worcestershire sauce
⅛ teaspoon pepper
    Dash of cayenne pepper
4 eggs
2⅓ cups milk
⅔ cup dry white wine*

Mix margarine, garlic and mustard; spread over bread slices. Cut each slice into thirds. Line bottom and sides of ungreased 8x8x2-inch baking dish with some of the bread slices, buttered sides down.

Mix cheese, onion, parsley, salt, Worcestershire sauce, pepper and cayenne pepper; spread over bread slices in dish. Top with remaining bread slices, buttered sides up. Beat eggs; mix in milk and wine. Pour over bread slices. Cover and refrigerate at least 2 hours.

Cook uncovered in 325° oven until knife inserted in center comes out clean, about 1¼ hours. Let stand 10 minutes before cutting.

9 servings.

*Wine can be omitted. Increase milk to 2½ cups.

PUFFY CHEESE BAKE

4 slices bread, buttered
2 eggs
1 cup half-and-half
2 tablespoons margarine or butter,
    melted
½ teaspoon salt
½ teaspoon dry mustard
¼ teaspoon paprika
    Dash of cayenne pepper
1½ cups shredded process American
    cheese (about 6 ounces)

Cut each slice bread into 4 triangles. Line bottom and sides of buttered 8x8x2-inch baking dish with bread triangles. (For a crown effect, place 8 triangles upright against sides of dish. Arrange remaining triangles in bottom of dish.) Beat eggs slightly; mix in remaining ingredients. Pour into baking dish. Cook uncovered in 350° oven until puffed and golden brown, about 40 minutes. Let stand 10 minutes before cutting.

4 servings.

CHEESE SANDWICH BAKE

1 package (10 ounces) frozen cut
    asparagus
¼ cup mayonnaise or salad dressing
1 small onion, chopped (about ¼ cup)
1 teaspoon prepared mustard
12 slices bread (crusts removed),
    toasted
6 slices American cheese
4 eggs, beaten
2½ cups milk
1 teaspoon salt
¼ teaspoon red pepper sauce

Cook asparagus as directed on package; drain. Mix mayonnaise, onion and mustard; spread over 6 slices toast. Arrange in ungreased 12x7½x2-inch baking dish. Top each slice toast in dish with 1 slice cheese. Spread asparagus over cheese. Place remaining slices toast on asparagus. Mix remaining ingredients; pour on top. Cook uncovered in 325° oven until knife inserted halfway between center and edge comes out clean, 1 to 1¼ hours.

6 servings.

CHEESE-SPINACH NOODLE CASSEROLE

2 cans (8 ounces each) tomato
    sauce
½ cup water
1 medium onion, chopped (about
    ½ cup)
1 clove garlic, finely chopped
¼ cup snipped parsley
1 teaspoon dried oregano leaves
½ teaspoon dried basil leaves
½ teaspoon salt
5 ounces uncooked green spinach
    noodles (3 to 3½ cups)
1 carton (12 ounces) creamed
    cottage cheese (small curd)
1½ cups shredded mozzarella or
    Swiss cheese (about 6 ounces)
⅓ cup grated Parmesan cheese

Heat tomato sauce, water, onion, garlic, parsley, oregano, basil and salt to boiling, stirring occasionally; reduce heat. Cover and simmer 10 minutes. Reserve ½ cup sauce; stir noodles into remaining sauce. Layer half each of the sauce-noodle mixture, cottage cheese and mozzarella cheese in ungreased 1½-quart casserole or 10x6x1½-inch baking dish; repeat. Top with reserved sauce. Cover and cook in 350° oven until noodles are tender, about 30 minutes. Sprinkle with Parmesan cheese. Cook uncovered 5 minutes longer.

6 servings.

Do-ahead Note: Before cooking, cover and refrigerate no longer than 24 hours. To serve, cook uncovered in 350° oven 45 minutes. Sprinkle with Parmesan cheese. Cook uncovered 5 minutes longer.

CHEESE-SPAGHETTI BAKE

1 package (7 ounces) thin spaghetti
¼ cup margarine or butter
¼ cup all-purpose flour
½ teaspoon salt
¼ teaspoon pepper
1 cup milk
1 cup water
1 teaspoon instant chicken bouillon
1 cup shredded Cheddar or process
    American cheese (about 4
    ounces)
3 hard-cooked eggs, chopped
⅓ cup sliced pimiento-stuffed olives
¼ cup grated Parmesan cheese

Cook spaghetti as directed on package; drain. Heat margarine in 3-quart saucepan over low heat until melted. Stir in flour, salt and pepper. Cook, stirring constantly, until smooth and bubbly; remove from heat. Stir in milk, water and instant bouillon. Heat to boiling, stirring constantly. Boil and stir 1 minute. Stir in Cheddar cheese, eggs and olives. Stir in spaghetti.

OVEN METHOD: Pour into ungreased 2-quart casserole or 12x7½x2-inch baking dish; sprinkle with Parmesan cheese. Cook uncovered in 350° oven until bubbly, 30 to 40 minutes.

RANGE-TOP METHOD: Reduce heat. Cover and simmer, stirring occasionally, until hot, 8 to 10 minutes. Sprinkle with Parmesan cheese.

6 servings.

Pictured at right: Pasta aplenty provides the starchy element in three delicious casseroles. Clockwise from top—Cheese-Spaghetti Bake (this page), Pepper, Macaroni and Cheese (page 84) and Cheese-Spinach Noodle Casserole (this page).

TOMATO, MACARONI AND CHEESE

 1 package (7 ounces) elbow
    macaroni
 ¼ cup chopped green onions (with
    tops)
 1 teaspoon salt
 1 teaspoon dry mustard
 ¼ teaspoon pepper
 2 tablespoons margarine or butter
 2 tablespoons all-purpose flour
 1½ cups milk
 4 cups shredded sharp Cheddar
    cheese (about 16 ounces)
 ½ cup grated Parmesan cheese
 2 tablespoons Worcestershire
    sauce
 2 large tomatoes, cut into ¼-inch
    slices
 ½ cup cracker crumbs
 2 tablespoons margarine or butter,
    melted

Cook macaroni as directed on package; drain. Cook and stir onions, salt, mustard and pepper in 2 tablespoons margarine in 2-quart saucepan over medium heat until onions are crisp-tender. Stir in flour. Cook over low heat, stirring constantly, until smooth and bubbly; remove from heat. Stir in milk. Heat to boiling, stirring constantly. Boil and stir 1 minute; remove from heat. Stir in Cheddar cheese, ¼ cup of the Parmesan cheese and the Worcestershire sauce until Cheddar cheese is melted. Stir in macaroni.

Layer half each of the macaroni mixture and tomato slices in ungreased 2-quart casserole or 12x7½x2-inch baking dish; repeat. Sprinkle with cracker crumbs. Drizzle with 2 tablespoons margarine; sprinkle with remaining Parmesan cheese. Cook uncovered in 375° oven until hot and bubbly, about 30 minutes.

6 servings.

■ To Microwave: Microwave 2 tablespoons margarine in 2-quart microwaveproof measure on high (100%) until melted, about 45 seconds. Stir in flour, salt, mustard and pepper. Stir in milk. Microwave, stirring every minute, until thickened, 4 to 5 minutes. Stir in Cheddar cheese, ¼ cup of the Parmesan cheese, the onions and Worcestershire sauce. Cover tightly and microwave until Cheddar cheese is melted, about 2 minutes. Stir in macaroni. Layer macaroni mixture and tomato slices as directed in 2-quart microwave-proof casserole; continue as directed. Cover loosely and microwave 5 minutes; rotate casserole ½ turn. Microwave until hot and bubbly, about 5 minutes.

MACARONI AND CHEESE

 1 to 1½ cups uncooked elbow
    macaroni, rigatoni or green
    spinach noodles (about 6
    ounces)
 ¼ cup margarine or butter
 1 small onion, chopped (about ¼
    cup)
 ½ teaspoon salt
 ¼ teaspoon pepper
 ¼ cup all-purpose flour
 1¾ cups milk
 8 ounces process sharp American
    or Swiss cheese or process
    cheese spread loaf, cut into ½-
    inch cubes

Cook macaroni as directed on package; drain. Cook and stir margarine, onion, salt and pepper in 2-quart saucepan over medium heat until onion is slightly tender. Stir in flour. Cook over low heat, stirring constantly, until smooth and bubbly; remove from heat. Stir in milk. Heat to boiling, stirring constantly. Boil and stir 1 minute; remove from heat. Stir in cheese until melted. Stir in macaroni. Pour into ungreased 1½-quart casserole or 10x6x1½-inch baking dish. Cook uncovered in 375° oven until hot and bubbly, about 30 minutes.

5 servings.

Olive, Macaroni and Cheese: Stir ¼ cup sliced ripe olives into cheese sauce. Arrange 1 large tomato, cut into 5 slices, around edge of casserole before cooking.

Pepper, Macaroni and Cheese: Stir ⅓ cup chopped green and/or red peppers or 1 can (4 ounces) chopped green chilies, drained, into cheese sauce. Reserve a few pepper slices for garnish if desired.

CHEESY LASAGNE

½ cup margarine or butter
½ cup all-purpose flour
½ teaspoon salt
4 cups milk
1 cup shredded Swiss cheese (about 4 ounces)
1 cup shredded mozzarella cheese (about 4 ounces)
½ cup grated Parmesan cheese
2 cups creamed cottage cheese (small curd)
¼ cup snipped parsley
1 teaspoon dried basil leaves
½ teaspoon salt
½ teaspoon dried oregano leaves
2 cloves garlic, crushed
12 uncooked lasagne noodles
½ cup grated Parmesan cheese

Heat margarine in 2-quart saucepan over low heat until melted. Stir in flour and ½ teaspoon salt. Cook, stirring constantly, until smooth and bubbly; remove from heat. Stir in milk. Heat to boiling, stirring constantly. Boil and stir 1 minute. Stir in Swiss cheese, mozzarella cheese and ½ cup Parmesan cheese. Stir over low heat until cheeses are melted. Mix cottage cheese, parsley, basil, ½ teaspoon salt, the oregano and garlic.

Spread ¼ of the cheese sauce mixture in ungreased 13x9x2-inch baking dish; top with 4 uncooked noodles. Spread 1 cup of the cottage cheese mixture over noodles; spread with ¼ of the cheese sauce mixture. Repeat with 4 noodles, the remaining cottage cheese mixture, ¼ of the cheese sauce mixture, the remaining noodles and the remaining cheese sauce mixture. Sprinkle with ½ cup Parmesan cheese. Cook uncovered in 350° oven until noodles are done, 35 to 40 minutes. Let stand 10 minutes before cutting.

12 servings.

CHEESE MANICOTTI

1 package (8 ounces) manicotti shells
1 package (10 ounces) frozen chopped spinach, thawed and drained
1 small onion, chopped (about ¼ cup)
1½ cups creamed cottage cheese
¼ cup grated Parmesan cheese
2 eggs
1 tablespoon instant chicken bouillon
½ teaspoon garlic powder
⅛ teaspoon dried thyme leaves
1 can (8 ounces) tomato sauce
1 cup shredded mozzarella cheese (about 4 ounces)

Cook manicotti shells as directed on package; drain. Mix spinach, onion, cottage cheese, Parmesan cheese, eggs, instant bouillon, garlic powder and thyme. Fill manicotti shells with spinach mixture; arrange in greased 13x9x2-inch baking dish. Pour tomato sauce over shells; sprinkle with mozzarella cheese. Cover and cook in 350° oven until hot, about 25 minutes.

5 servings.

ZUCCHINI AND TOMATO

3 eggs
½ cup milk
½ cup buttermilk baking mix
1 teaspoon salt
¼ to ½ teaspoon cayenne pepper
¼ teaspoon pepper
3 cups chopped zucchini
3 cups chopped tomatoes
2 cups shredded Cheddar cheese (about 8 ounces)

Beat eggs, milk, baking mix, salt, cayenne pepper and pepper. Place zucchini in buttered 8x8x2-inch baking dish; sprinkle with tomatoes and cheese. Pour egg mixture over cheese. Cook uncovered in 350° oven until golden brown, 45 to 50 minutes. Let stand 10 minutes before cutting.

6 servings.

CHEESE-ONION BAKE

2 medium onions, thinly sliced
1 small green pepper, chopped
    (about ½ cup)
1 jar (4 ounces) sliced mushrooms,
    drained
2 tablespoons margarine or butter
2 cups buttermilk baking mix
¾ cup milk
1 egg
2 cups shredded Swiss cheese
    (about 8 ounces)
¾ cup dairy sour cream
1 egg
½ teaspoon salt

Cook and stir onions, green pepper and mushrooms in margarine until tender. Mix baking mix, milk and 1 egg; spread in greased 9x9x2-inch pan. Spread onion mixture on top; sprinkle with cheese. Mix remaining ingredients; pour on top. Cook uncovered in 400° oven until golden, 30 to 35 minutes.

6 servings.

CHEESE-TOMATO PIE

1 cup shredded Cheddar cheese
    (about 4 ounces)
1 cup shredded mozzarella cheese
    (about 4 ounces)
1 cup shredded Monterey Jack
    cheese (about 4 ounces)
1 medium onion, chopped (about
    ½ cup)
2 tablespoons all-purpose flour
4 eggs
1 cup milk
½ teaspoon salt
½ teaspoon dry mustard
½ teaspoon Worcestershire sauce
2 medium tomatoes, sliced

Mix cheeses, onion and flour. Spread in greased 10x1½-inch pie plate or 9-inch quiche dish. Beat eggs slightly; beat in milk, salt, mustard and Worcestershire sauce. Pour over cheese mixture. Bake in 350° oven until set, 35 to 40 minutes. Let stand 10 minutes. Arrange tomato slices around edge of pie.

8 servings.

ENCHILADA CASSEROLE

2 cups shredded Monterey Jack
    cheese (about 8 ounces)
1 cup shredded Cheddar cheese
    (about 4 ounces)
1 medium onion, chopped (about
    ½ cup)
½ cup dairy sour cream
2 tablespoons snipped parsley
1 teaspoon salt
¼ teaspoon pepper
1 can (15 ounces) tomato sauce
⅔ cup water
⅓ cup chopped green pepper
1 tablespoon chili powder
½ teaspoon dried oregano leaves
¼ teaspoon ground cumin
1 clove garlic, finely chopped
8 tortillas
¼ cup shredded Cheddar cheese

Mix Monterey Jack cheese, 1 cup Cheddar cheese, the onion, sour cream, parsley, salt and pepper; reserve. Heat tomato sauce, water, green pepper, chili powder, oregano, cumin and garlic to boiling, stirring occasionally; reduce heat. Simmer uncovered 5 minutes. Pour into ungreased 8 or 9x1¼-inch pie plate.

Dip each tortilla into sauce to coat both sides. Spoon about ¼ cup cheese mixture onto each tortilla; roll tortilla around filling. Arrange in ungreased 12x7½x2-inch baking dish. Pour remaining sauce over enchiladas. Sprinkle with ¼ cup Cheddar cheese. Cook uncovered in 350° oven until hot and bubbly, about 20 minutes. Garnish with dairy sour cream and chopped onions or lime wedges if desired.

4 to 5 servings.

Do-ahead Note: After sprinkling with cheese, cover and refrigerate no longer than 24 hours. To serve, cook uncovered in 350° oven about 35 minutes.

SOUTHERN BAKED BEANS

6 cups water
1 pound dried white marrow or navy beans (about 2 cups)
¾ pound lean salt pork or smoked pork, sliced
1 medium onion, chopped (about ½ cup)
2 cloves garlic, finely chopped
½ teaspoon red pepper sauce
1 bay leaf, crumbled
¼ cup catsup
¼ cup molasses
1½ teaspoons dry mustard
½ teaspoon salt
½ teaspoon ground ginger
1½ teaspoons Worcestershire sauce
⅓ cup packed dark brown sugar

Heat water and beans to boiling; boil 2 minutes. Remove from heat; cover and let stand 1 hour.

Stir in pork, onion, garlic, pepper sauce and bay leaf. Heat to boiling; reduce heat. Cover and simmer until beans are tender, 1½ to 2 hours (do not boil or beans will burst). Drain beans, reserving liquid. Add enough water to bean liquid, if necessary, to measure 2 cups.

Pour bean mixture into ungreased 2-quart casserole. Stir catsup, molasses, mustard, salt, ginger and Worcestershire sauce into reserved bean liquid; pour over beans. Arrange pork on top; sprinkle with brown sugar. Cook uncovered in 400° oven 1 hour.

6 servings.

BAKED SOYBEANS

6 cups water
1 pound dried soybeans (about 1 cup)
1 teaspoon salt
1 medium stalk celery, chopped (about ½ cup)
1 medium onion, chopped (about ½ cup)
1 small green pepper, chopped (about ½ cup)
¼ cup packed brown sugar
¼ cup vegetable oil
3 tablespoons dark molasses
1 teaspoon dry mustard
½ teaspoon salt

Heat water and soybeans to boiling in Dutch oven; boil 2 minutes. Remove from heat; cover and let stand 1 hour.

Add 1 teaspoon salt to beans and water. Heat to boiling; reduce heat. Cover and simmer about 2 hours. (Add more water during cooking if necessary.) Stir in celery, onion and green pepper; simmer about 1 hour longer. Drain beans, reserving liquid. Add enough water to reserved bean liquid, if necessary, to measure 1½ cups.

Pour bean mixture into ungreased 2-quart casserole. Mix reserved bean liquid, the brown sugar, oil, molasses, mustard and ½ teaspoon salt; stir into bean mixture. Cook uncovered in 400° oven until hot and bubbly, about 1 hour.

6 to 8 servings.

ITALIAN-STYLE BAKED BEANS

4 cups water
1 pound dried lima or Great
    Northern beans (about 2 cups)
2 teaspoons salt
2 tablespoons margarine or butter
¾ cup chopped onion
¾ cup chopped green pepper
1 clove garlic, finely chopped
1 can (6 ounces) tomato paste
½ cup sliced pitted ripe olives
¼ cup grated Parmesan cheese
2 to 3 teaspoons chili powder
1 teaspoon salt

Heat water and beans to boiling; boil 2 minutes. Remove from heat; cover and let stand 1 hour.

Add enough water to beans to cover if necessary. Add 2 teaspoons salt. Heat to boiling; reduce heat. Cover and simmer until tender, 45 to 60 minutes (do not boil or beans will burst). Drain beans, reserving liquid. Add enough water to bean liquid, if necessary, to measure 1 cup.

Heat margarine in 10-inch skillet until melted. Add onion, green pepper and garlic; cook and stir until onion is tender. Mix in beans, reserved bean liquid and the remaining ingredients. Pour into ungreased 2-quart casserole. Cook uncovered in 375° oven until hot and bubbly, about 30 minutes.

6 servings.

Pictured at left: Cheese Manicotti (page 85), Italian-style Baked Beans (above) and Egg and Wild Rice Casserole (page 77) prove that eggs, cheese and beans are all good—and delicious—sources of protein.

SAUSAGE-BEAN CASSEROLE

4 cups water
1 pound dried Great Northern or
    navy beans (about 2 cups)
1½ pounds pork boneless shoulder
1 pound link sausage, cut into
    1-inch pieces
6 slices bacon, cut into 2-inch
    pieces
4 medium carrots, sliced
2 medium onions, sliced
2 cloves garlic, chopped
2 bay leaves
1 can (6 ounces) tomato paste
2 teaspoons salt
½ teaspoon dried thyme leaves
½ teaspoon dry mustard
¼ teaspoon pepper
    Snipped parsley

Heat water and beans to boiling in Dutch oven; boil 2 minutes. Remove from heat; cover and let stand 1 hour.

Add enough water to beans to cover if necessary. Heat to boiling; reduce heat. Cover and simmer until almost tender, about 1½ hours (do not boil or beans will burst). Drain beans, reserving liquid.

Trim fat from pork; cut pork into ¾-inch cubes. Cook and stir pork, sausage and bacon over medium heat until brown; drain. Place beans, meat mixture, carrots, onions, garlic and bay leaves in ungreased 4-quart bean pot, casserole or Dutch oven.

Add enough water to reserved bean liquid to measure 2 cups. Mix reserved liquid, the tomato paste, salt, thyme, mustard and pepper; pour over beans. Add water to almost cover mixture. Cover and cook in 325° oven, stirring occasionally, 1 hour. Uncover and cook until beans are desired consistency, about 30 minutes. Remove bay leaves. Garnish with parsley.

8 servings.

BAKED LIMAS WITH CARROTS

4 cups water
1 pound dried baby lima or Great Northern beans (about 2 cups)
½ pound salt pork, cut into ¼-inch pieces
1 medium carrot, chopped (about ½ cup)
1 medium onion, chopped (about ½ cup)
¼ teaspoon pepper

Heat water and beans to boiling; boil 2 minutes. Remove from heat; cover and let stand 1 hour.

Heat to boiling; reduce heat. Simmer uncovered until beans are almost tender, 25 to 30 minutes (do not boil or beans will burst). Drain beans, reserving liquid.

Cook and stir pork in 10-inch skillet until golden brown; drain, reserving ¼ cup fat. Mix fat, beans, carrot, onion and pepper; spread in ungreased 12x7½x2-inch baking dish. Add enough reserved bean liquid to cover. Sprinkle pork over top. Cover and cook in 350° oven until vegetables are tender, 40 to 50 minutes. Sprinkle with snipped parsley if desired.

6 to 8 servings.

Dealing with Dried Beans

Dried beans have a tendency to foam during the first cooking. To prevent this, add a tablespoon of oil or shortening, or if the water in your area is very hard, add ⅛ to ¼ teaspoon baking soda for each cup of beans. Later, cook slowly over low heat. To test beans for doneness, simply pierce a bean with the tip of a knife. What about leftover dried beans? You can store them in a tightly covered container 6 to 8 months. Cooked dried beans can be stored in the refrigerator up to 4 days or in the freezer up to 3 months.

BEAN AND HOMINY BAKE

1 package (10 ounces) frozen sliced okra
1 can (30 ounces) kidney beans, drained
1 can (20 ounces) hominy, drained
1 can (16 ounces) whole tomatoes
2 medium stalks celery, thinly sliced
1 tablespoon Worcestershire sauce
½ teaspoon salt
⅛ teaspoon dried dill weed
1½ cups shredded cheese (about 6 ounces)
2 tablespoons imitation bacon

Rinse frozen okra under running cold water to separate; drain. Mix okra, beans, hominy, tomatoes (with liquid), celery, Worcestershire sauce, salt and dill weed in ungreased 2-quart casserole; break up tomatoes with fork. Sprinkle with cheese. Cook uncovered in 350° oven until hot and cheese is melted, about 30 minutes. Sprinkle with imitation bacon.

6 servings.

MEXICAN-STYLE BEAN BAKE

1 can (17 ounces) refried beans
1 medium onion, finely chopped (about ½ cup)
1 small green pepper, finely chopped (about ½ cup)
4 eggs
1½ cups shredded Cheddar cheese (about 6 ounces)
1 teaspoon chili powder
⅛ teaspoon garlic powder
1 jar (12 ounces) salsa

Mix beans, onion, green pepper, eggs, ¾ cup of the cheese, the chili powder and garlic powder. Pour into ungreased 9x9x2-inch pan; sprinkle with remaining cheese. Cook uncovered in 350° oven until hot and firm, about 30 minutes. Heat salsa, stirring occasionally, until hot; serve with bean bake.

6 servings.

BEAN AND CORN BREAD CASSEROLE

2 cans (21 ounces each) baked beans
2 cans (15 ounces each) kidney
    beans, drained
1 can (8½ ounces) lima beans,
    drained
1 can (8 ounces) tomato sauce
¼ cup catsup
2 tablespoons packed brown sugar
2 tablespoons instant minced onion
½ teaspoon dry mustard
½ teaspoon salt
¼ teaspoon pepper
   Corn Bread Topping (below)

Heat oven to 425°. Mix all ingredients except Corn Bread Topping. Pour into ungreased 13x9x2-inch baking dish. Prepare Corn Bread Topping. Spoon evenly over bean mixture to within 1 inch of edges. Cook uncovered until topping is golden brown, 25 to 30 minutes.

8 servings.

CORN BREAD TOPPING

⅔ cup all-purpose flour
⅓ cup cornmeal
1 tablespoon sugar
1 teaspoon baking powder
½ teaspoon salt
1 egg
½ cup milk
2 tablespoons margarine or butter,
   softened

Beat all ingredients with hand beater until smooth.

BEAN AND RICE CASSEROLE

1 pound bulk pork sausage
2 medium stalks celery, sliced
   (about 1 cup)
1 medium onion, chopped (about
   ½ cup)
2 cups cooked brown or regular rice
1 can (15 ounces) kidney beans,
   drained
1 can (16 ounces) whole tomatoes
1 teaspoon dried oregano leaves
1 teaspoon salt
½ teaspoon dried savory leaves
¼ teaspoon pepper
½ teaspoon red pepper sauce
1 cup shredded Monterey Jack
   cheese (about 4 ounces)

Cook and stir sausage, celery and onion in 10-inch skillet over medium heat until sausage is brown, 10 to 15 minutes; drain. Stir in rice, beans, tomatoes (with liquid) and the remaining ingredients except cheese; break up tomatoes with fork. Pour into ungreased 2-quart casserole. Cook uncovered in 350° oven 30 minutes. Sprinkle with cheese. Cook uncovered until cheese is melted, about 5 minutes longer.

6 servings.

PORK SAUSAGE-BEAN CASSEROLE

¾ pound bulk pork sausage
1 can (21 ounces) baked beans
½ cup catsup or chili sauce
⅛ teaspoon pepper
1 red apple, thinly sliced
2 to 4 tablespoons packed brown
   sugar

Cook and stir sausage in 10-inch skillet until light brown; drain. Stir in beans, catsup and pepper. Pour into ungreased 1½-quart casserole or 10x6x1½-inch baking dish. Arrange apple slices on top; sprinkle with brown sugar. Cook uncovered in 400° oven until hot and bubbly, 25 to 30 minutes.

4 or 5 servings.

BAKED BEANS WITH FRANKFURTERS

2 cans (16 ounces each) baked beans
1 package (12 ounces) frankfurters, cut into ½-inch slices
1 small onion, chopped (about ¼ cup)
1 tablespoon prepared mustard
1 teaspoon celery salt

OVEN METHOD: Mix all ingredients in ungreased 2-quart casserole or 8x8x2-inch baking dish. Cover and cook in 350° oven until hot and bubbly, about 30 minutes.

RANGE-TOP METHOD: Mix all ingredients in 3-quart saucepan. Heat over medium heat, stirring occasionally, until hot, about 8 minutes.

5 servings.

■ **To Microwave:** Mix all ingredients in 2-quart microwaveproof casserole. Cover tightly and microwave on high (100%) 5 minutes; stir. Cover and microwave until hot, 4 to 6 minutes longer.

THREE-BEAN CASSEROLE

1 package (10 ounces) frozen lima beans
1 can (21 ounces) baked beans
1 can (15½ ounces) kidney beans, drained
½ pound Italian or pork link sausages
1 small onion, chopped (about ¼ cup)
½ cup catsup
1 tablespoon packed brown sugar
½ teaspoon salt
½ teaspoon dry mustard
⅛ teaspoon pepper

Cook lima beans as directed on package; drain. Mix lima beans, baked beans and kidney beans in ungreased 2-quart casserole. Heat sausages and small amount water to boiling; reduce heat. Cover and simmer 5 minutes; drain. Cook sausages until brown on all sides (do not prick sausages). Cut each sausage into 2 or 3 pieces; stir into beans. Mix remaining ingredients; stir into bean mixture. Cook uncovered in 400° oven until hot and bubbly, 40 to 50 minutes.

6 servings.

Ham-Bean Casserole: Substitute ¾ cup cut-up fully cooked smoked ham or ¼ cup imitation bacon for the cooked sausages.

Index

B
Bacon-cheese macaroni, 34
Baked beans. *See* Bean(s).
Baked crab and shrimp, 71
Baked limas with carrots, 90
Baked soybeans, 87
Barley
  beef, casserole, 19
  curried lamb and, casserole, 39
Bean(s). *See also* Green bean(s).
  and corn bread casserole, 91
  and hominy bake, 90
  and rice, beef with, 22
  and rice casserole, 91
  baked, Italian-style, 89
  baked, Southern, 87
  baked, with frankfurters, 92
  baked limas with carrots, 90
  baked soybeans, 87
  dried, about, 90
  ham-, casserole, 92
  Mexican-style, bake, 90
  pork sausage-, casserole, 91
  sausage-, casserole, 89
  three-, casserole, 92
Beef. *See also* Ground beef.
  and beans, Mexican, 20
  and corn casserole, 26
  and vegetable casserole, 23
  barley casserole, 19
  beer stew, 27
  Burgundy, 19
  Cantonese, 20
  dried, casserole, 25
  hash, 24
  liver casserole, 26
  oven stew, 22
  -potato scallop, 22
  -sausage rolls, 24
  slices with vegetables, 25
  steak and kidney pie, 23
  stew, winter, 19
  with beans and rice, 22
Beer stew, 27
Biscuits, chicken and, 52
Bologna-noodle-bean bake, 38
Bratwurst
  sausage and sauerkraut, 37
Bread crumbs, making, 71

Broccoli
  -beef squares, 13
  -cheese bake, 79
  chicken-, casserole, 41
  classic turkey divan, 58
Brown rice
  orange chicken with, 42
  sausage-, casserole, 35

C
Canadian bacon and zucchini
    bake, 32
Cheese
  bacon-, macaroni, 34
  bake, puffy, 81
  broccoli-, bake, 79
  buying, 31
  chili-zucchini casserole, 79
  confetti rice casserole, 78
  -egg bake, 79
  enchilada casserole, 86
  ham 'n bake, 31
  impossible cheeseburger pie,
    14
  lasagne, 35
  lasagne, cheesy, 85
  lasagne, no-noodle, 14
  macaroni and, 84
  manicotti, 85
  'n chilies oven omelet, 76
  olive, macaroni and, 84
  -onion bake, 86
  pepper, macaroni and, 84
  pie, impossible chilies-, 77
  puff on creamed chicken, 50
  sandwich bake, 81
  -spaghetti bake, 82
  -spinach noodle casserole, 82
  storing, 64
  strata, 81
  strata, double, 80
  strata, Spanish, 80
  three-, medley, 80
  tomato, macaroni and, 84
  -tomato pie, 86
  -topped beef pie, 16
  zucchini and tomato, 85
Cheesy eggs and mushrooms, 75
Cheesy lasagne, 85

Chicken
  almond casserole, 48
  and biscuits, 52
  and curry sauce, 44
  and dressing, 45
  and hominy casserole, 53
  -asparagus bake, 54
  breasts with rice, 42
  -broccoli casserole, 41
  broth, equivalents for, 47
  cacciatore casserole, 47
  cooked, yields for, 52
  creamed, and corn bread, 52
  creamed, cheese puff on, 50
  dinner casserole, 48
  festive, 46
  -green bean casserole, 54
  livers and rice, 55
  -macaroni casserole, 49
  Mexican-style, 44
  'n stuffing bake, 53
  orange, with brown rice, 42
  puff, 53
  salad, hot, 54
  -spinach casserole, 47
  tetrazzini, 49
  with macaroni, oven, 45
  with phyllo, 50
Chili
  with macaroni, 11
  -zucchini casserole, 79
Chilies
  cheese 'n, oven omelet, 76
  -cheese pie, impossible, 77
Chinese pork and rice, 28
Chop suey casserole, 7
Clam
  spaghetti, 74
  squares with shrimp sauce,
    74
Classic turkey divan, 58
Cod and vegetable bake, 60
Confetti rice casserole, 78
Corn bread
  bean and, casserole, 91
  creamed chicken and, 52
Corned beef
  hash, 24
  'n noodle casserole, 25

Crab(meat)
  and shrimp, baked, 71
  bake, Dixie, 73
  pie, impossible, 65
  puff, 71
  spinach noodle-, casserole, 72
Cranberry whirls over turkey, 58
Creamed chicken and corn
      bread, 52
Croutons, making, 71
Crunchy beef-noodle casserole,
    10
Crunchy fish-noodle casserole,
    59
Crunchy tuna casserole, 68
Curried beef and rice, 7
Curried lamb and barley
    casserole, 39
Curried shrimp casserole, 70
Curried tuna casserole, 62

D
Deep dish turkey pie, 57
Dixie crab bake, 73
Double cheese strata, 80
Dried beef casserole, 25
Dumplings, ham and, 32

E
Easy oven spaghetti, 12
Egg(s)
  and chips, 78
  and mushrooms, cheesy, 75
  and rice casserole, 76
  and wild rice casserole, 77
  au gratin casserole, 78
  cheese-, bake, 79
  cheese 'n chilies oven omelet,
    76
  confetti rice casserole, 78
  hard-cooking, 79
  impossible chilies-cheese pie,
    77
  oven omelet, 76
  spinach oven omelet, 76
  turkey and, casserole, 56
  Western casserole, 75
Enchilada casserole, 86

F
Festive chicken, 46
Fish. *See also* Salmon; Tuna.
  bake, saucy, 60
  casserole, Greek style, 59
  cod and vegetable bake, 60
  Hawaiian halibut, 60
  -noodle casserole, crunchy, 59
  spinach noodle-seafood
    casserole, 72

Frankfurter(s)
  baked beans with, 92
  frank-macaroni pie, 34
  -noodle casserole, 34
  zucchini and franks, 34

G
Green bean(s)
  chicken-, casserole, 54
  -mushroom medley, 10
  -tomato medley, 10
Ground beef
  beef and eggplant casserole, 9
  beef and macaroni, 11
  beef and potato strata, 13
  beef manicotti, 12
  broccoli-beef squares, 13
  cheese-topped beef pie, 16
  chili with macaroni, 11
  chop suey casserole, 7
  crunchy beef-noodle casserole,
    10
  curried beef and rice, 7
  easy oven spaghetti, 12
  green bean-mushroom medley,
    10
  green bean-tomato medley, 10
  hearty beef casserole, 8
  impossible cheeseburger pie,
    14
  lasagne, 35
  layered tostada bake, 17
  meatballs with mixed
    vegetables, 18
  Mexicali spoon bread
    casserole, 16
  moussaka, 39
  no-noodle lasagne, 14
  popover-topped beef, 17
  stroganoff deep dish pie, 17
  taco casserole, 14
  Texas hash, 8

H
Haddock
  Hawaiian halibut, 60
Halibut, Hawaiian, 60
Ham
  and dumplings, 32
  and eggplant au gratin, 30
  -bean casserole, 92
  layered, dinner, 31
  'n cheese bake, 31
  popover, 30
Hash
  beef, 24
  corned beef, 24
  Texas, 8
Hawaiian halibut, 60

Hearty beef casserole, 8
Herbs, fresh, substitutions for,
    26
Hot chicken salad, 54

I
Impossible cheeseburger pie, 14
Impossible chilies-cheese pie, 77
Impossible crabmeat pie, 65
Impossible shrimp pie, 65
Impossible tuna pie, 65
Italian-style baked beans, 89

L
Lamb
  and barley casserole, curried,
    39
  casserole, 38
  moussaka, 39
  stew, 40
Lasagne, 35
  cheesy, 85
  no-noodle, 14
  tuna, 64
Layered ham dinner, 31
Layered tostada bake, 17
Luncheon meat
  pork 'n sweet potato casserole,
    29

M
Macaroni
  and cheese, 84
    olive, 84
    pepper, 84
    tomato, 84
  bacon-cheese, 34
  beef and, 11
  chicken-, casserole, 49
  chicken with, oven, 45
  chili with, 11
  dried beef casserole, 25
  frank-, pie, 34
  salmon 'n spaghetti, 70
  shrimp casserole, curried, 70
  tuna-, casserole, 63
  tuna-pasta bake, 62
  yields, 63
  zucchini and franks, 34
Manicotti
  beef, 12
  cheese, 85
Meatballs with mixed vegetables,
    18
Mexicali spoon bread casserole,
    16
Mexican beef and beans, 20
Mexican-style bean bake, 90
Mexican-style chicken, 44

Microwave recipes
  baked beans with frankfurters, 92
  beef casserole, hearty, 8
  beef hash, 24
  chicken and hominy casserole, 53
  chicken breasts with rice, 42
  chicken-broccoli casserole, 41
  chicken dinner casserole, 48
  chicken-green bean casserole, 54
  chicken macaroni casserole, 49
  chicken 'n stuffing bake, 53
  chicken salad, hot, 54
  chili with macaroni, 11
  corned beef 'n noodle casserole, 25
  crab and shrimp, baked, 71
  dried beef casserole, 25
  eggs and chips, 78
  fish bake, saucy, 60
  fish-noodle casserole, crunchy, 59
  green bean-mushroom medley, 10
  green bean-tomato medley, 10
  ham dinner, layered, 31
  meatballs with mixed vegetables, 18
  pork 'n noodle casserole, 29
  pork 'n sweet potato casserole, 29
  sausage-brown rice casserole, 35
  shrimp casserole, curried, 70
  spaghetti, easy oven, 12
  Texas hash, 8
  tomato, macaroni and cheese, 84
  tuna and chips, 67
  tuna casserole, curried, 62
  tuna chow mein casserole, 67
  tuna-cracker casserole, 67
  tuna-rice bake, 62
  turkey and egg casserole, 56
  turkey divan, classic, 58
  turkey-rice casserole, 56
Moussaka, 39

N
No-noodle lasagne, 14
Noodle(s). *See also* Spinach noodle.
  -bean bake, bologna-, 38
  corned beef 'n, casserole, 25
  crunchy beef-, casserole, 10
  frankfurter-, casserole, 34

Noodles *(continued)*
  oysters and, deluxe, 73
  pork 'n, casserole, 29
  Romanoff, salmon, 63
  Romanoff, tuna, 63
  yields, 63

O
Olive, macaroni and cheese, 84
Onion, chopped fresh, substitutions for, 26
Orange chicken with brown rice, 42
Oriental-style lamb casserole, 40
Oriental-style veal casserole, 40
Oven chicken with macaroni, 45
Oven omelet, 76
Oven stew, 22
Oyster(s)
  and noodles deluxe, 73
  spaghetti, 74

P
Pepper, macaroni and cheese, 84
Phyllo, chicken with, 50
Pie
  cheese-tomato, 86
  cheese-topped beef, 16
  deep dish turkey, 57
  frank-macaroni, 34
  impossible cheeseburger, 14
  impossible chilies-cheese, 77
  impossible crabmeat, 65
  impossible shrimp, 65
  impossible tuna, 65
  steak and kidney, 23
  stroganoff deep dish, 17
Pizza bake, spicy, 37
Popover
  ham, 30
  sausage and vegetable, 37
  -topped beef, 17
Pork. *See also* Ham; Sausage.
  and rice, Chinese, 28
  bacon-cheese macaroni, 34
  beer stew, 27
  Canadian bacon and zucchini bake, 32
  chop and potato casserole, 27
  chops with fruited rice, 28
  'n noodle casserole, 29
  'n sweet potato casserole, 29
  sausage-bean casserole, 89
Pork sausage-bean casserole, 91
Poultry, cooked, yields for, 52
Puffy cheese bake, 81

R
Rice. *See also* Brown rice; Wild rice.
  bean and, casserole, 91
  beef with beans and, 22
  chicken breasts with, 42
  chicken livers and, 55
  Chinese pork and, 28
  confetti, casserole, 78
  cooking, 55
  curried beef and, 7
  egg and, casserole, 76
  fruited, pork chops with, 28
  tuna-, bake, 62
  turkey-, casserole, 56
  yields, 55

S
Salmon
  'n spaghetti, 70
  -noodles Romanoff, 63
  -potato casserole, 69
  soufflé, 69
Sandwich bake, cheese, 81
Saucy fish bake, 60
Sausage
  and sauerkraut, 37
  and vegetable popover, 37
  bean and rice casserole, 91
  -bean casserole, 89
  beef-, rolls, 24
  -brown rice casserole, 35
  lasagne, 35
  pork, -bean casserole, 91
  spicy pizza bake, 37
Seafood. *See also specific kind.*
  spinach noodle-, casserole, 72
Shrimp
  crab and, baked, 71
  curried, casserole, 70
  pie, impossible, 65
  puff, 71
Smoked beef
  beef and corn casserole, 26
Smoked chicken
  chicken-asparagus bake, 54
Smoked turkey
  chicken-asparagus bake, 54
Soufflé
  salmon, 69
  tuna, 69
Southern baked beans, 87
Soybeans, baked, 87
Spaghetti
  cheese-, bake, 82
  chicken tetrazzini, 49
  clam, 74
  easy oven, 12
  oyster, 74

Spaghetti *(continued)*
  salmon 'n, 70
  -tuna casserole, 64
  tuna 'n, 70
  yields, 63
Spanish strata, 80
Spicy pizza bake, 37
Spinach noodle
  cheese-, casserole, 82
  -crab casserole, 72
  -seafood casserole, 72
Spinach oven omelet, 76
Spoon bread casserole, Mexicali, 16
Steak and kidney pie, 23
Stew
  beer, 27
  lamb, 40
  oven, 22
  winter beef, 19
Stroganoff deep dish pie, 17

T
Taco casserole, 14
Texas hash, 8
Three-bean casserole, 92
Three-cheese medley, 80
Tomato, macaroni and cheese, 84

Tostada bake, layered, 17
Tuna
  and chips, 67
  -asparagus casserole, 65
  chow mein casserole, 67
  -cracker casserole, 67
  crunchy, casserole, 68
  curried, casserole, 62
  lasagne, 64
  -macaroni casserole, 63
  'n spaghetti, 70
  noodles Romanoff, 63
  -pasta bake, 62
  pie, impossible, 65
  -potato puff, 68
  -potato scallop, 68
  -rice bake, 62
  soufflé, 69
  -spaghetti casserole, 64
Turkey
  and egg casserole, 56
  chicken and biscuits, 52
  chicken and hominy casserole, 53
  chicken-green bean casserole, 54
  chicken 'n stuffing bake, 53
  chicken puff, 53

Turkey *(continued)*
  cooked, yields for, 52
  cranberry whirls over, 58
  creamed chicken and corn bread, 52
  divan, classic, 58
  hot chicken salad, 54
  pie, deep dish, 57
  -rice casserole, 56
  wild rice and, casserole, 56

V
Veal casserole, Oriental-style, 40

W
Western casserole, 75
Wild rice
  and turkey casserole, 56
  egg and, casserole, 77
Winter beef stew, 19

Z
Zucchini
  and franks, 34
  and tomato, 85
  Canadian bacon and, bake, 32
  chili-, casserole, 79
  no-noodle lasagne, 14